TWAYNE'S WORLD AUTHORS SERIES

A Survey of the World's Literature

Sylvia Bowman, Indiana University

GENERAL EDITOR

NORWAY

Leif Sjöberg, State University of New York, Stony Brook

EDITOR

Johan Borgen

(TWAS 311)

Johan Borgen

Johan Borgen

By RANDI BIRN

University of Oregon

Twayne Publishers, Inc.   ::   New York

Library of Congress Cataloging in Publication Data

Birn, Randi.
  Johan Borgen.

  (Twayne's world authors series, TWAS 311. Norway)
  Bibliography: p. 167.
  1. Borgen, Johan, 1902–
PT8950.B713Z6   839.8'2'372   73-23114
ISBN 0-8057-2167-3

For Ray,
Eric and Laila

Contents

Preface

For nearly half a century Johan Borgen has been a central figure in Norwegian cultural life. He is an accomplished journalist, critic, and social commentator who, through frequent appearances on Norwegian radio, has become widely known to an audience with little direct access to his writings. In his literary undertakings Borgen has attempted every genre, including poetry. In the 1930's he wrote plays in a manner later associated with Ionesco and the postwar avant-garde in France. Nevertheless, it is in his short stories and novels that Borgen truly excels. As a novelist he matured slowly. His breakthrough came with the first volume of the *Lillelord* trilogy in 1955, a full thirty years after his debut as a prose writer. Between 1955 and 1972 Borgen published a series of extraordinary novels, and it is safe to say that these works and the short stories will determine his place in the realm of Scandinavian letters. While many of the themes in the mature fiction appear in his earlier works, it is in the later novels that Borgen fully develops these themes and ultimately resolves the conflicts upon which his fiction is based. I have chosen to concentrate my study upon the mature work and short stories because it is through them that the author's intentions are most fully comprehended and his significance most clearly grasped.

My method is a textual analysis, and I have refrained from using biographical information for the purpose of illuminating a given work or apparent change in the author's attitude toward his characters and their problems. My study explores recurring character types, images, and themes in the hope of achieving a deeper understanding of Borgen's overall corpus. How, for instance, does the quest for a father in *Lillelord* relate to Peter Holmgren's search for a mountaintop in *Blåtind*, or Frank Vegårdshei's obsession with a caged gorilla in *Min arm, min tarm*? What is the significance of the recurring images of mutilated children? Or of the small volumes that so many Borgen protagonists carry in their pockets?

My study reveals that Borgen's mature fiction is remarkably coherent. In fact, each of the novels essentially treats aspects of a single basic problem—that of the conflicting forces which pull the hero between a subjective quest for identity and an outward movement toward others. It is the conflict between psychological solitude and social solidarity. All of Borgen's important sub-themes—the sense of lost identity, the fragmentation of the personality, and the quest for innocence and wholeness—are intimately related to the basic conflict within the protagonist's personality. While each novel represents an attempt at solving the conflict, the entire corpus unveils an evolutionary pattern—from mysticism, through faith in knowledge and artistic vision, through disenchantment, and finally toward resolution through concrete involvement in the world.

There exists in Borgen's work an interesting correlation between form and meaning. The form of the *Lillelord* trilogy is diffuse and ambitious, the work of an author virtually overwhelmed by the richness of his own material. Nevertheless, it is a highly appropriate way of relating the torment of Wilfred Sagen, a protagonist literally ripped apart by conflicting urges. The esthetically superior novels *"Jeg"* and *Den røde tåken* reflect varying degrees of faith in the artistic vocation and acceptance of a poetic solution to the problems of life. On the other hand, *Blåtind* betrays a sense of intense doubt, illustrated by agonized dialogues among the main characters. I found this novel, which has not been a critical success, of crucial importance in understanding Borgen's total production. Conversely, the simple, realistic structure of *Min arm, min tarm* nicely complements the way in which Frank Vegårdshei resolves his underlying problems.

Since the themes which concern Borgen belong within the mainstream of contemporary literature, I have tried to point out certain similarities between his work and that of several internationally known writers. While the direct influence of Hamsun and Kafka is very strong, I also have indicated less direct affinities between Borgen and certain French-language authors who have contributed toward defining the individual's plight in the modern world. The sense of personality fragmentation and quest for esthetic wholeness have a Proustian ring, the conflict between the self and others bears resemblance to Sartre and the Existentialists, the struggle against arid intellectualism brings to mind the anti-heroes of Samuel Beckett. The concern for form in *"Jeg"* and *Den røde tåken* resembles the formalism of the French "new novel." I realize of course that to a certain extent the parallels I underscore are based upon personal background and inclination—and that for Proust, Sartre, and Beckett I might have selected Hemingway, Faulkner, and Virginia Woolf. My purpose, however, is to be suggestive rather than exhaustive. Borgen's characters are steeped in the Western literary heritage, and their relationship to this heritage is intimately related to the central problems of his work. In fact, one may state that Borgen's entire career is a prolonged struggle for liberation from his heritage. This is precisely what Frank, the protagonist in *Min arm, min tarm,* accomplishes when he abandons the Romantic approach toward life.

To date, Borgen has been the subject of very little critical work. That no book on him exists probably is due to the belief of critics that he has not yet said his final word. From 1955 to 1972 novels and short stories kept appearing in rapid succession. While Borgen undoubtedly will continue to write until the end of his life, I consider *Min arm, min tarm* to represent the culmination of a long quest. In fact, it is a plateau from which one may experience an overview of Borgen's literary career. The essays and articles which exist on Borgen are chiefly concerned with single works of his, or else briefly compare themes in a few of his novels. Most notably, Kjell Heggelund discusses the conflict between reality and fiction in *"Jeg,"* while Kjell Berger concentrates upon the thematic unity between *"Jeg"* and the *Lillelord* trilogy.[1] Somewhat more general in nature is the essay by Leif Longum, who cites Borgen's place within contemporary Norwegian fiction.[2] Willy Dahl's remarks on Borgen in *Stil og struktur* are quite suggestive, but as in Longum's case Dahl's interest does not focus upon Borgen but rather upon the broader spectrum of Norwegian letters.[3] The articles written on Borgen suggest the need for a comprehensive study. Translations into English of *Lillelord* and *Den røde tåken* currently are under way, and I do not veil my hope that a critical analysis such as this, in English, will point out the need to make this exceptional novelist and short-story writer more accessible to those unable to read Norwegian. In my bibliography I realize that I may have omitted some valuable critical material. I beg a certain amount of indulgence for this fact, as I have had to compose most of my manuscript far from Scandinavia and the sources located there. In a few cases the lack of library facilities dictated my choice of editions.

I am especially grateful to Leif Sjöberg, editor of Twayne's series on Scandinavian authors, for his unremitting encouragement in the preparation of the manuscript; to Ingrid Weatherhead, who read much of the manuscript in rough first draft and offered excellent advice—especially on translating Borgen's prose into English; to Johan Borgen himself, for his cooperation was invaluable; finally to my husband, Raymond Birn, who has been a devoted partner in the preparation of each stage of my study. His demands for clarity, logic, and improvements in style occasionally exasperated us both. Nevertheless, if my book is readable, above all it is thanks to him.

RANDI BIRN

University of Oregon

Chronology

1902   Johan Borgen born April 28 in Oslo to an established lawyer's family. Attended "Frøknene Platous forskole" and "Frogner skole," both private schools.

1920   Took the *eksamen artium.*

1923   Began career as part-time journalist for the Oslo daily *Dagbladet.*

1925   *Mot mørket* (*Towards Darkness*). Short stories.

1926   Spent several months in Paris. Traveled through France on bicycle.

1928–   Full-time columnist for *Dagbladet.*
1941

1932   *Betraktninger og anfektelser* (*Observations and Temptations*). Collection of *Dagbladet* columns.

1934   Married Annemarta Evjenth. Two daughters and one son born of the marriage. *Når alt kommer til alt* (*When All Is Said and Done*). Novel.

1936   *Kontorsjef Lie* (*Executive Lie*). Play. *Seksti Mumle Gåsegg* (*Sixty Mumle Gåsegg*). Collection of *Dagbladet* columns.

1937   Traveled on a Norwegian cargo ship to the West Coast of North America. Prolonged stay in Southern California. Traveled by bus through the Pacific Coast states and Western Canada. *Barnesinn* (*The Child's Mind*). Short stories. *Høit var du elsket* (*Dearly Were You Loved*). Play.

1938   *Mens vi venter* (*While We're Waiting*). Play.

1940   *Andersens* (*Andersen's*). Play.

1941   Arrested in mid-September by the Germans in occupied Norway and sent to the Grini prison camp near Oslo.

1942   Released from Grini in March. Worked for the Resistance.

1943   Fled Norway into neutral Sweden.

1944   *Ingen sommar* (*No Summer*). Novel. In Swedish.

1945   *Dager på Grini* (*Days at Grini*). Memoir. *Nordahl Grieg.* Biography of the poet. Became Norwegian press attaché in Copenhagen.

1946   *Kjærlighetsstien* (*Love Lane*). Novel. *Ingen sommer* (*No Summer*). Norwegian version.

1947– Worked as stage director in Oslo and several provincial towns.
1959 Directed over forty plays.
1947 *Akvariet (The Aquarium)*. Play. Visit to Russia.
1948 *Hvetebrødsdager (Honeymoons)*. Short stories. Traveled on Norwegian cargo ship through Mediterranean to the Middle East.
1949 *Jenny og påfuglen (Jenny and the Peacock)*. Novel. *Vikinger og eventyr (Vikings and Fairy Tale)*. Two plays.
1952 *Noveller om kjærlighet (Love Stories)*. Short stories. Traveled in France, Italy, and Austria.
1954– Editor of the literary journal *Vinduet*.
1959
1954 *Natt og dag (Night and Day)*. Short stories.
1955 *Lillelord (Little Lord)*. Novel.
1956 *De mørke kilder (The Dark Springs)*. Novel.
1957 *Vi har ham nå (We Have Him Now)*. Novel.
1959 *"Jeg" ("I")*. Novel.
1959– Lived in London. Worked for West Croyden Theatre.
1960
1960 *Innbilningens verden (The World of Imagination)*. Reflections on art.
1961 *Noveller i utvalg, 1936–1961 (Selected Short Stories, 1936–1961)*. Co-winner in the international short-story contest sponsored by *The New York Herald Tribune*. Winning story "Elsk meg bort fra min bristende barndom" ("Release Me Through Love From My Crumbling Childhood").
1963 *Frigjøringsdag (Day of Liberation)*. Play originally written in English.
1964 *Blåtind (Blue Peak)*. Novel.
1965 *Barndommens rike (The Land of Childhood)*. Autobiography. Contents previously broadcast over Norwegian radio in fifteen installments. *Nye noveller (New Short Stories)*. Awarded Nordisk Råd's annual literary prize.
1966 *Ord gjennom år (Words Through the Years)*. Collected journalism and radio broadcasts. *Innbilningen og kunsten (Imagination and Art)*. Revised version of *Innbilningens verden*.
1967 *Bagateller (Trifles)*. Stories. *Den røde tåken (The Red Mist)*. Novel.
1968 *Alltid på en søndag (Always on a Sunday)*. Sixty radio talks.
1969 *Trær alene i skogen (Trees Alone in the Forest)*. Short stories.
1970 *Elsk meg bort– (Release Me–)*. Stories. Borgen settled permanently at Hvaler near Fredrikstad.

Chronology

1971   *Mitt hundeliv (My Dog Days)*. Stories. *129 Mumle Gåsegg.* Collection of *Dagbladet* columns 1930–1941.

1972   *Min arm, min tarm (My Arm, My Intestine)*. Novel. Borgen became the winner of a national short-story contest sponsored by the journal *Samtiden*. See "Desembersol" ("December Sun"), *Samtiden,* LXXXI, 8, 469–82.

1973   *Den store havfrue (The Large Mermaid)*. Novel.

CHAPTER 1

Borgen's Career

JOHAN Borgen was born on April 28, 1902, the youngest of four sons in a comfortable, bourgeois Oslo family. His father was a respected, well-established attorney. The childhood Borgen recalls was a privileged one, associated with "light and good food and all friendly things."[1] The Borgen family divided its time between a spacious villa in the capital and a summer residence on an island in the Oslo Fjord. It was a world of maids in starched aprons and caps, sumptuous family dinners, and anticipated visits to the theater. The environment was not a particularly literary one, but the family library contained the familiar Norwegian and Danish classics as well as the masterpieces of world literature in French, German, and English. Danish, nevertheless, was the significant literary language of Borgen's childhood, and this has always been important for him. Today, in his seventies, he remains very close to contemporary trends in Danish literature; and along with Hamsun, Kafka, Hemingway, and Faulkner, it is the Danish writers H. C. Andersen, Herman Bang, and H. C. Branner to whom he acknowledges his strongest debt.

Borgen's childhood combined that doting protectiveness and recreational liberty peculiar to Norwegian upper-class life in the early twentieth century. He discovered the public library before he was old enough to get his own circulation card, and he recalls standing next to the check-out counter poring through novels he still was too young to take home. Johan and his brothers attended "Frøknene Platous forskole," an exclusive private school in the capital, where opportunities were rare for contact with children from a social milieu vastly differing from their family's. Nevertheless, the boy's existence was not a sheltered cocoon. At the age of six, accompanied only by a little friend, Johan Borgen already was making ski

17

excursions into Oslo's Frogner Park. The boys carried their own
rucksacks containing sandwiches and hot drinks, and they would
pass their time together in the half-light of a January morning.
Subsequently Johan's explorations took him into the poor en-
claves that dotted the upper-class neighborhoods of the city.
He discovered the underprivileged, alcoholism, and a rawness
and brutality of life that would turn him away from the
condescending conservatism of his class. When he was ten,
Borgen received a bicycle from his parents. Now the entire
city was open to him, then its suburbs, and even neighboring
towns. In the company of a friend, the ten-year-old would
pack a lunch and ride out as far as Drammen, fifty miles away.

Borgen recalls the bicycle as having offered him a first opportunity to experience the immense variety of nature and
humans. It was a vehicle leading to genuine freedom and independence. In *Barndommens rike* he observes: "In his time
Zola wrote—alas, so naively—that nothing like the bicycle gives
man the sensation of flying through the air. I agree with Zola.
I flew, I was delighted. During the night I would awaken and
think: the bicycle! And my joy would become so intense that
I would have to get up and dance on the floor, and then
whimper."[2] In his twenties the bicycle continued to enrapture
him. It was his principal means of transportation during trips
through Denmark and France.

Borgen recalls his first twelve years with extraordinary gusto
and nostalgia. Every excursion was an adventure, on foot, on
skis, but especially on his bicycle. He always remained grateful
to his parents for the liberty he enjoyed in childhood, for their
"forgetting" in the morning the empty wine glasses that had
been left only half empty the evening before, for their having
permitted him, at the age of ten, to ferry a party of guests
back to the mainland in the middle of the night.

He links the idyll of childhood with the exuberance of the new
nation, born in 1905 with the beginning of the reign of Haakon
VII. For himself and for Norway the outbreak of World War I
coincided with the end of the period of carefree existence.
In 1914 innocence ceased being a virtue. While the Norwegian
government maintained a strict neutrality, the English blockade
and German submarine warfare dragged the small nation into

the conflict. Hundreds of Norwegian sailors perished, and more than a few businessmen profiteered. For Borgen World War I represented a coming of age for Norway, a loss of innocence, a "fall." Many of the protagonists in Borgen's fiction pass from childhood during 1914–18. Almost uniformly, their essential aim in life is to return to the state of innocence, a condition that Borgen associates with the life that he cherished prior to the cataclysm.

During his youth Johan Borgen accepted most of the social views of his family. Except for his father, the Borgens were arch-conservative. Even *Aftenposten*, the Conservative Party newspaper, was too liberal for certain family members. The atmosphere at home was always open, and healthy disagreement tolerated. In a patrician sense the elder Borgen was an active spokesman for penal reform, the assumption by society of responsibilities toward the poor, and liberty of expression. On the other hand, both parents scorned the tactics of the English suffragettes and were convinced that the eight-hour workday and paid vacations would weaken immeasurably the moral fiber of the nation. However, young Johan veered more and more closely toward the left, and told his parents so. The family bonds were resilient enough to withstand the strain of Johan's politics; and later in life, when Marxism had its greatest appeal for him, Borgen resolutely maintained his affection for the environment of his parents' home. The imprint of this environment has left a very deep mark. A certain inborn conservatism, a patrician's libertarianism, pervades his social thought. He has little faith in material progress and is no friend of the welfare state. He is an ardent individualist and places the highest premium upon authentic personal happiness. He is aware of the paradoxical nature of certain of his ideas and calls himself a radical and reactionary rolled into one.

In the early 1920's, however, it was the radical side that came to the forefront. Having taken his *eksamen artium* in 1920, he broke with the traditional habit of his class by forsaking the university or the business world for a job as a part-time reporter on the irreverent liberal Oslo daily *Dagbladet*. Eight years later he took up his famous column "Mumle Gåsegg." Even in the tolerant atmosphere of the Borgen household, Johan's act must have smacked of class betrayal. Borgen recalls an ancient parrot, belonging to a family friend, who, to the delight of all, was taught to repeat over and over: "You're reading *Dagbladet*? Then go to hell!"[3] But Borgen's association with *Dagbladet* was of immense value to him. His tasks were not confined to reporting. As Erling Nielsen notes, "He wrote about films, reviewed books (an average of fifty per year), reported everything from royal jubilees to campaigns for moral decency, composed feature articles, wrote great quantities of weekly portraits, and did the layout for the evening edition."[4] A colleague described Borgen as "one of the most energetic, restless, working journalists I have ever known."[5] At the daily staff meeting Borgen was the person to whom all turned in quest of new ideas, and he generously offered them. He was devoted to journalism. In order to get his many tasks done, Borgen was forced to adopt a working tempo that has become legendary. He would compose very rapidly, rarely needing to rewrite. His habits have carried through into his fiction. He made the transition from feature article to short story without difficulty. However, he was fifty-four before his first critically successful novel, his first genuinely sustained effort, was published. One cannot state with certainty that his development as a journalist delayed his maturity as a novelist. But it is useful to note that one of the most essential themes in Borgen's fiction is the longing for contemplative pauses, during which the individual may free himself from overbusy routine in order to ask significant questions about his own existence.

As a journalist Borgen traveled considerably in Scandinavia. In 1926 he took an extended trip to France. He lived for several months in Paris, took note of the existence of America's lost generation there, and toured the countryside by bicycle. It was another eleven years before he again voyaged far from Scandinavia. In 1937 he and his wife booked passage on a Norwegian freighter and sailed through the Panama Canal before docking on the west coast of the United States. He bussed through Oregon, Washington, and British Columbia, toured California, and spent some time in Hollywood.

In his column for *Dagbladet* Borgen chose as his pen name "Mumle Gåsegg." The original is an insatiable, irritating character who appears in the Norwegian folktales compiled by Asbjørnsen and Moe.[6] Borgen's prewar columns ranged all over, from lyrical descriptions of nature, recollections from his travels, and mild social satire, to meditations upon literature and the problem of lost identity. At the age of twenty-three Borgen published his first volume of fiction, a collection of short stories called *Mot mørket* (*Towards Darkness*), 1925. He was already concerned with themes that would characterize his mature writing, namely, the problems of personal and social alienation and the quest for authenticity. Hamsun was his inspiration, a fact that provoked a crisis in his artistic development. So steeped was he in Hamsun's work that he found himself unable to formulate a literary style of his own. He discovered that his efforts were becoming nothing but pastiches of his master, and he therefore gave up creative writing for nearly a decade.

Borgen recalls quite poignantly the paralyzing influence Hamsun had upon him when he was just beginning his literary career. He sees himself at that time as a youth striving for liberty, but fundamentally powerless to tear himself loose from the idol that he worshiped. The result was a poisoning of his talent, and to this day he deplores his own "unhappy talent for imitation." From 1928 to 1934, *Dagbladet* occupied nearly all his time. When he returned to creative writing, he composed a novel, *Når alt kommer til alt* (*When All Is Said and Done*), 1934. In time, of course, maturity brought an ability to fend for himself, Borgen located his own style, and Hamsun became a distinctly positive source of inspiration.

The protagonist in *Når alt kommer til alt* is an individual whose inability to face the problems of everyday reality causes him to drift into a world of dreams which are shortly transformed into nightmares. The protagonist ultimately discovers that dream leads to oblivion and death, and he therefore makes an attempt to reestablish his foothold in the real world. His will to make a commitment to the real fails him, however, and at the novel's conclusion he once more turns away from reality in order to escape into a new dream. The difficulty of making choices—what Borgen calls the Hamlet problem—dominates this early work. The problem has a central place in the play *Mens vi venter* (*While We're Waiting*), which was published in 1938, as well as in all of Borgen's mature novels.

As with most of Borgen's contemporaries in Norwegian literary and intellectual life, the problem of making choices came easily enough after April, 1940. For the second time in his life Borgen saw the conflicts among the Great Powers wrench his country from its comparative isolation and self-proclaimed neutrality—and on this occasion the wrenching was particularly brutal. For more than a year after the start of the German occupation Norwegian journalism was not completely stifled by censorship and propaganda. Borgen continued to write for *Dagbladet,* though his skills as a satirist were already being put to the test. The butt of his humor was the invader, and the postwar edition of *129 Mumle Gåsegg* (1971) reveals clearly in retrospect his inventiveness and talents.

But by the autumn of 1941 Borgen was considered a dangerous enough character, and a direct challenge to the censor landed him a stay at Grini, the most notorious internment camp the Germans established for Norwegians. In contrast to the prison camps for foreigners in Norway, not to mention the death factories that dotted the rest of Europe, Grini was—at least for a time—a rather innocuous place. Discipline was lax, most prisoners enjoyed a good deal of liberty within the confines of the camp, their spirit remained intact, and packages from concerned relatives were smuggled in regularly. While there, Borgen enjoyed the company of the leaders of prewar Norwegian intellectual life. His fellow prisoners included Harald Grieg, director of Gyldendal, the country's most important publishing house; Professor Francis Bull, the famous Ibsen scholar at the University of Oslo; and Arnulf Øverland, the poet and political agitator. In *Dager på Grini* (*Days at Grini*), 1945, Borgen portrays the camp as a Stalag 17 for the intelligentsia. Since the chief sport of the inmates was maintenance of their moral superiority over their captors, wit's triumph over force is a basic theme running through the memoir. In the spring of 1942, however, the German occupation of Norway assumed a form built upon terror, and of course Grini felt the brunt of the new policy. Torture and selections for deportation to Germany became common. During an interview with a camp officer in March, 1942, that he knew was decisive, Borgen wondered until the end whether his fate would be a German death camp or restoration to his family. He was sent home, became active in the Resistance, and had to flee to Sweden in 1943. While in hiding in Oslo prior to his escape he wrote *Far, mor og oss* (*Father, Mother, and Us*), humorous stories from childhood; during his stay in Sweden he published *Ingen sommar* (*No Summer*), a novel.

Ingen sommar was first translated into Swedish and later published in Norwegian, in 1946. It was Borgen's first novel in ten years and only the second he had published in a literary career dating back to 1925. Its central focus is the effect that a shared crisis, the war, may have on the individual crises of a group of people. The war experience renders the Hamlet theme nearly meaningless. National catastrophe whittles down the fact of choice. An upper-class girl, a middle-aged prostitute, an artist in quest of identity, and the latter's psychiatrist find that their personal problems no longer matter. Facing the common enemy, each individual locates his place within the Resistance.

Ingen sommer (its Norwegian title) is of course something of a period piece. One nevertheless can sense Borgen's exultation over the sense of common purpose he discovered among his countrymen caught in the net of the occupation. In Borgen's mature fiction, the duality between solitude and solidarity with others will form a significant theme. With the Liberation, however, came the inevitable disillusionment. The heroic qualities that had seemed so appealing from 1940 to 1945 disappeared. Society seemed to sink back into mediocrity, selfishness born of deprivation replaced the sense of community, and the nation seemed to be floundering in quest of its lost will. Borgen's first postwar novel, *Kjærlighetsstien* (*Love Lane*), 1946, reflected his disillusioned mood. The book is a satire directed against bourgeois convention. Its location is a middle-sized Norwegian town after the end of the war, and Borgen treats social groups rather than individuals. His pockets of characters incorporate the town fathers representing the governing class, the *nouveaux riches*, shopkeepers, workers, and prostitutes. A simple formula sets apart the positive from the negative characters. Cutting through the center of town is a controversial street. This is "Kjærlighetsstien," where the prostitutes live and work. "Kjærlighetsstien" represents an honest, open approach toward life. Individuals from the different social milieus frequent the street, but only those who approach it without shame or guilt are the sympathetic characters. These characters most often derive from the lower social groups and are politically attracted to socialism and communism. On the other hand, those who visit "Kjærlighetsstien" covertly or who condemn the activities occurring there exhibit a moral hypocrisy that Borgen associated with political conservatism, anti-communism, and sympathy for fascism. While Borgen's formula appears oversimple, the mood at the end betrays disillusionment. Two of the "good" characters perish; Mr. Andersen, the author's *porte-parole*, has a doomsday vision; the headquarters for a group of Neo-Nazis burns down but immediately is invaded by rats.

For a time after the war Borgen flirted with communism, and he made a trip to Russia in 1947. But the rigidity of any type of social dogma struck against the grain of a profound libertarianism, and he preferred to approach political and social circumstances unfettered by ideological restraints. He continued to contribute articles and reviews to *Dagbladet,* but did not return to the newspaper as a full-time journalist. He devoted more time to the theater and in 1954 undertook the editorship of the lively literary periodical *Vinduet.* He remained on *Vinduet* for six years. Though *Vinduet* occupied large periods of his time and he traveled the length of Norway producing plays for the many amateur theater groups that dot the country, Borgen spent the greater part of the postwar years cultivating the short story and the novel.

Since the publication of *Barnesinn* (*The Child's Mind*) in 1937 no doubt has ever existed as to Borgen's exceptional gifts as a short-story writer. He subsequently published seven additional volumes beginning with *Hvetebrødsdager* (*Honeymoons*) in 1948. In 1961 Borgen shared first prize in *The New York Herald Tribune*'s international short-story competition, and four years later his collection *Nye noveller* (*New Short Stories*) won *Nordisk Råds litteraturpris,* next to the Nobel Prize the most coveted literary award in Scandinavia. On the other hand,

Borgen's breakthrough as a major novelist occurred late. *Når alt kommer til alt* and *Ingen sommer* were not critical successes, and skeptics wondered whether Borgen indeed could sustain himself in a longer narrative than the short story. In the mid-1950's, however, Borgen composed the trilogy that was to establish his reputation. It is a work of epic proportions published in consecutive years—*Lillelord* (*Little Lord*), 1955 *De mørke kilder* (*The Dark Springs*), 1956; and *Vi har ham nå* (*We Have Him Now*), 1957. The trilogy covers the life of Wilfred Sagen, a character who is born with the century and who commits suicide on Liberation Day, May 8, 1945. In the background of the period covered by Wilfred's life is the spiritual development of twentieth-century Norway. The *Lillelord* volumes are ambitious and complex, and the trilogy has enjoyed an excellent critical reception. It is considered one of the most significant contributions to the postwar Scandinavian novel.

Two years after the publication of *Vi har ham nå*, Borgen had another surprise in store—an experimental novel, *"Jeg"* (*"I"*), 1959. This work parted markedly in form from anything Borgen previously had written. Of all his novels, *"Jeg"* remains Borgen's favorite.[7] Puzzled by its structure, some reviewers received it with polite reservations. Unkinder ones found it contrived and went so far as to call it a pastiche of Kafka. However, serious critics such as Leif Longum and Kjell Heggelund find *"Jeg"* to be a novel of great importance.[8] In 1960 Borgen's own essay *Innbilningens verden* (*The World of Imagination*) provided an account of the esthetic philosophy upon which the writer's production is built. The essay is indispensable for an understanding of Borgen's fiction, especially *"Jeg"* and his subsequent novels *Blåtind* (*Blue Peak*), 1964, and *Den røde tåken* (*The Red Mist*), 1967.

Past seventy, and in frail health, Borgen shows no signs of retirement. Late in 1972 his eleventh novel appeared, *Min arm, min tarm* (*My Arm, My Intestine*), an analysis of a schizophrenic's efforts to reintegrate his personality and reestablish contact with reality. From 1965 to 1969 Borgen also published *Barndommens rike*, a set of childhood recollections; *Trær alene i skogen* (*Trees Alone in the Forest*), yet another collection of short stories; and *Alltid på en søndag* (*Always on a Sunday*), a compilation of sixty brief radio talks.[9] After spending most of his life in Oslo, in 1970 Borgen moved permanently to a large country manor at Hvaler, on an island halfway down the Oslo Fjord, near Fredrikstad. The house is accessible only by sea or a primitive path. The automobile cannot reach it. Hvaler nevertheless is customarily filled with visitors and grandchildren. One has the feeling that it is here, surrounded by sea and forest, family and friends, that Borgen has found the most appropriate environment in which to come to terms with the esthetic problem that suffuses his entire corpus, the problem of human authenticity.

CHAPTER 2

Journalist and Critic

I *Mumle Gåsegg*

BORGEN is a born satirist. Pillars of society, the family, condescending humanitarians, statesmen defending national honor, and purveyors of the blessings of the consumer society are the principal victims of his wit. The satirical edge to Borgen's novels occasionally leaves the reader wondering whether the hero's eccentric behavior is to be taken at face value. Is Borgen serious, or is he putting us on? On several occasions we never seem to know. As a journalist, writing a regular column in *Dagbladet* for thirteen years, Borgen cultivated a technique that turned his "mumle gåsegg" into a national institution. Nothing is as dated as yesterday's syndicated column. Nevertheless, a collection of Borgen's articles from 1930 to 1941, published in paperback a generation later, reads with surprising freshness.[1] Those who knew the subject matter at first hand quickly recall the events commented upon. Those for whom the events have little personal significance can grasp, through Borgen's prose, the passions that were inspired. The original Mumle Gåsegg was a kind of Nordic Pantagruel, who on emerging from the egg, immediately cried out for herring, soup, porridge, and milk. He was endlessly resourceful, totally irreverent, and irrepressible. Borgen could not have chosen a more appropriate pen name.

Borgen is also a born moralist, and each of his columns was intended to make his reader think in terms of moral issues. He saw himself as a catalyzing agent and illustrated his function in a description of a grandfather, written for *Dagbladet* in the early days of World War II:

"Oh yes," sighed Grandfather, and he leaned back in the rocking chair.—"So it is starting to get darker again."

27

He is funny that way, Grandfather, he knows how to achieve his effects. After he had said that, he said no more. He just leaned back in the chair and left it up to us to think what we wanted. Yes, just as a single push of his rocker liberated the energy of that technological wonder, and it continued to rock rhythmically for a long, long time, so too it must have been his intention that our thoughts should be set into motion, liberated by his simpleminded little remark.[2]

Often the "mumle gåsegg" had a brief cast of characters. The first was Borgen himself, the working journalist who interviewed foreign dignitaries at nine and had to listen to the complaints of irate citizens at ten. Prewar Oslo was a cozy, provincial town, and *Dagbladet*—with its muckraking reputation—kept its office doors open. Anyone with a gripe about the Establishment was welcome, for a good story might have the most prosaic source. In a column entitled "Around the Event" Borgen revealed to his readership the problems besetting him in his many-sided job.[3] The year is 1936, and he just learned that the German pacifist Carl von Ossietzky had belatedly won the 1935 Nobel Peace Prize. Many construed this award as a direct slap at Hitler by the Nobel Committee. While the columnist is mulling over the political consequences of the event, thinking of the interviews he now must arrange, an Oslo burgher enters his office and drones on about walking conditions in the city's main street. The delightful *dialogue des sourds* seems straight out of Ionesco:

"Can you tell me," said the man, "why the sidewalk on one side of Karl Johan is always so wet, while the other side is quite dry?"

"No," we said, focusing our glance an instant upon the person entering. "Perhaps you know it: Ossietzky has won the Nobel Peace Prize!"

"Has he really," said the stranger. "Excuse me if I sit down for a moment. You see, I fell in the street."

"At this moment," we prated on absent-mindedly while arranging telephone interviews with prominent women and men who might have a word to say about the occasion, ". . . at this moment the announcement is being broadcast around the world. At this moment, for instance, Goebbels is learning about it. Has it struck you how he must look?"

"It was as if I had been struck down," said the intruder, who by now had taken a seat. "Let me tell you, now that it is getting so cold in the morning these wet sidewalks certainly are something. One has to feel his way along. It makes no sense at all."[4]

The dialogue is a little masterpiece. Though the reporter and his unwanted visitor completely fail to strike up lines of communication, for the thoughtful reader their disjointed "conversation" has a significance. The journalist surmises aloud: "Had Ossietzky received the Peace Prize for 1935 in 1935, much suffering might have been avoided." The man from the street responds: "Yes, and damaging effects too. Not to mention damaging effects. There are people who suffer shocks from such a fall. You should have seen how slippery it was." Indeed, the world is a slippery place in 1936. Ethiopia, Bolivia, Paraguay, Spain, and even Germany seem to be worlds apart from the wet streets of Oslo. Nations and ideals are toppling. Nothing can be more certain than the long-term shocks involved.

In addition to the journalist, two other characters appear frequently in the "mumle gåsegg" columns. The first is Mrs. Johansen, the proprietor of a well-stocked delicatessen. The second is Little Inger, an inquisitive ten-year-old. The forthrightness and simple clarity of Mrs. Johansen represent what Borgen considers the most attractive traits of the Norwegian personality. She punctures hypocrisy and has no use for either moral flabbiness or deceit. Little Inger employs her child's naiveté with similar effect. No other party can escape the unmerciful logic of her questioning. For example, perplexed by the government's mysterious sale of ammunition to another country, she asks her parents:

"Which foreign country is supposed to get these bullets then?"

"Nobody knows that," said Father. "What is essential is that the country is not at war, and it says in the paper that it isn't."

"But what if it had been at war?" said Inger.

"Well, then we could not have sent those bullets," said Father. "You know, Inger, that one cannot support a country at war like that. It's immoral."

"But what if they got into a war?" said Inger.

"Yes," Mother replied. "That is precisely why they must have the bullets, you understand. For if there will be a war, then they will need them."

"Won't it be immoral then?" said Inger.

And as a final blow to the reasoning of her parents, the little girl adds:

> "One had better keep watching," said Inger.
> "Nonsense," said Father. "What is one supposed to watch?"
> "When those countries aren't at war. So we can get our bullets sold," said Inger. (Jan. 19, 1937)[5]

Borgen's prewar articles have a familiar ring. They covered themes ranging from criticism of the inferior status of women to the consumer-oriented society. The denial of individuality, the plight of the artist, and mistreatment of petty criminals concerned him deeply. Above all, it was the deteriorating political situation in Europe that disturbed him most. Torn between a sincere antimilitarism and despair over the weaknesses of the democracies before the totalitarian menace, Borgen confessed his dilemma in his columns. On the one hand, he berated the English for building ammunition factories in Scotland and Wales (March 2, 1937); and on the other, through Mrs. Johansen, he scorned the attempts of diplomacy to maintain the peace. In a column dated August 6, 1938, he describes how he once tried to address Mrs. Johansen as a diplomat would in making his purchases. His profession of excessive *politesse* enraged her, and she lifted her carving knife menacingly. Then, pulling herself together, she addressed him:

> "You are insane," Mrs. Johansen said calmly, placing the salami on her wonderful machine that cuts a medium-thick slice with each turn.
> "Insane? Don't you realize that this is the official means of communication between the appointed representatives of friendly peoples when they wish to assure each other their lasting respect and wishes for eternal peace?"
> . . . . . .
> Mrs. Johansen calmly wrapped the merchandise into two sheets of paper, one transparent and one white, whereupon she added up her slanting numbers.
> "I shall tell you one thing," she said. "When they speak like that there will be WAR."[6]

From 1938 on Borgen's pacifism gave way to dismay over the complacency he saw around him as the dictatorships became increasingly belligerent. In a column he describes the behavior of a gay theater crowd in Oslo on the evening following Hitler's Nuremberg address on German intentions for Czechoslovakia (September 14, 1938). The blazing, semicomprehensible newspaper headlines clash with the mood of the people, a mood built upon an evening's entertainment, a drink, late dinner, and dancing. By focusing upon tiny elements like a cigarette left burning a hole in the leather glove of one of the theatergoers, Borgen lays stress upon the suppressed tension in the air and the hollow nature of the crowd's joy. There is anticipation of the worst, fears for the future. Once the evening is finished, ". . . once the fingers have turned off the lamp on the night stand, and the edge of the down quilt is drawn snugly and comfortably up to the tip of the nose—then it is there again: the wire service message, the newspaper on display. And from this moment on, there are images, horrible images, appearing in rapid succession, refusing to stop, something from a film.

"At last we are awake."[7]

Neither Mrs. Johansen nor Little Inger shares the popular jubilation over the Munich accords. "She is no optimist, Mrs. Johansen," notes the journalist. As for Little Inger, considerably older and considerably more disillusioned than at the time when she used to put Mother and Father on the spot, the world has become a place where only cynics can retain their sanity. She notes that in 1938 Eduard Beneš will be paying the price for the Nobel Peace Prize, and someone else will be paying it in 1939.[8] Ethiopia and Spain already are behind us. Now if only the Czechs can keep their mouths shut. "To be brief, now we want peace," says Inger's uncle. "Lock the door and turn on the dance music" (September 30, 1938).[9]

When war came to Poland, and Norway struggled for some additional months of precious neutrality, Borgen's columns forsook satire for concrete descriptions of the climate of fear that had settled over the land. Hope, even false hope, no longer was in the air, only a waiting for the day when the dagger would strike home: "If we think correctly, everything around us reveals sorrow and darkness. And it will become worse." People desperately look for a way to assume their regular pattern of existence. The unpleasant experiences of everyday life, such as the arrival of an unwanted bill, are accompanied by a sigh of relief—for they tell us that despite the nightmare out there things are normal. An envelope arrives in the mail. "You are torn from your dream and grasp it eagerly. Beneath your hands it sparkles in a familiar and pleasant manner, and you think: Thank heavens, only a bill!" (January 12, 1940).[10]

But on April 9, 1940, the nightmare assumed reality. Oslo awoke to the rhythm of German troops marching up Karl Johansgate. The occupation of Norway was to last until May, 1945. For a year and a half, until he was shipped off to Grini, Borgen continued to write his "mumle gåsegg." His wartime pieces are particularly interesting, the overwhelming number related in some fashion or other to the occupation—some veiled in allegory, but others quite straightforward, escaping the irregularly applied censorship. Sorrow, astonishment, bewilderment, encouragement, even pleas for direct action, are the prevailing sentiments of the pieces. Just prior to Borgen's imprisonment, the censorship became particularly brutal; and the journalist reverted to animal stories and seemingly lyrical accounts of nature. In nearly every article, however, at least one sentence would refer to the wartime situation. Borgen wished to make certain that no reader missed the point of the "mumle gåsegg" now—to support the spirit of resistance in the minds of the Norwegian people.

Borgen's piece for April 10, 1940, the day following the German invasion, is almost a prose poem. The authenticity of the emotions felt reminds one of Aragon's poems of the occupation in France. On the beautiful spring day, Borgen notes, everyone displays his sorrow, but the deepest misery is carried in the heart: "It is within you, like a tight piece of armor beneath the skin. And you cannot remove it."[11] The article "Publicity Release for a Map" (May 1, 1940) reflects the disbelief of Norwegians upon discovering that their isolated ribbon of land suddenly has become a centerpiece in world events. In time, however, it will fade into the background, along with Ethiopia, Spain, and Finland. Borgen looks at the map of Norway he just has pinned to his wall, and he recalls the maps of other martyred countries that had hung there in recent years: "Later you took down the maps, one by one. Contours that had

been burned into you gradually became vague; names whose
significance once had seemed eternal again became empty
sounds, nothing but consonants that stuck on the tongue."[12]
The article was written during the counterattack of the British,
French, and Norwegians in the north of the country. Borgen
holds no illusions about the outcome of hostilities. "No, down
they must come, the maps, down from the wall. Up with the
next one, and down with that too." Norway will slip from
memory, evaporating "along with the steam of Finland's dark
swamps, with the dust clouds along the railway from Djibouti
to Addis Ababa."

"Publicity Release for a Map" is not an especially accurate
reflection of Borgen's general mood during the first year of the
occupation. Despair did not become him. By way of contrast,
"In Number Ten" (June 5, 1940) elicits an air of defiance. He
is paying his customary call upon Mrs. Johansen, and she greets
him cynically: "So, you're still alive?" The remark has a special
significance, since the piece appeared in the first number of
Dagbladet that followed a period of suppression.[13] The journalist
asks for some salami, and Mrs. Johansen inquires whether he
would like the peppered kind. He hesitates, and she repeats
her question as an open challenge: "Well, do you want it
peppered?" The journalist responds: "Lady, we are among
countrymen here. The salami is supposed to be peppered." Borgen
thus promises his readership strong, spicy meat despite the
consequences. There is, as both Ragnar Vold and Erling Nielsen
point out, an added meaning. Some years previously Quisling
had been waylaid and beaten up. Pepper was thrown into his
eyes. Borgen reveals his intention of pursuing a strident tone
as long as he can.

Still, most of Borgen's articles were of necessity less con-
tentious than "In Number Ten." Certain of the most effective
ones vividly described the mood in Oslo during the summer,
fall, and winter of 1940–41. They were symbolic as well, written
in such a way as to be fully comprehensible to a public aware
of Borgen's moral purpose. For example, "Sigh in the Night"
(April 13, 1940) describes the attempts of individuals to orient
themselves in the unrelieved darkness of the city. Quite clearly
Borgen has the collectivity of the nation in mind as well, seeking

a means of steadying itself in face of the night that had fallen
upon the land. "At Half Moon" (April 15, 1940) and "When
They Meet" (April 7, 1941) reveal the importance of the radio
in offering the groups settled around it their links to the outside
world, and at the same time preventing them from sinking back
into a false complacency.

Borgen's use of allegory was hardly very subtle, and, in retrospect, it is a wonder that he stayed out of Grini as long as he
did. His article "About Bears" (October 17, 1940) describes an
invasion by the beasts who leave a trail of destruction in their
path. The following year it is serpents, sharks, and other un-
savory creatures that are filling Norway's seas and forests
(July 22, 1941). In the piece entitled "About Mushrooms"
(June 20, 1941) he warns his readers to be exceedingly cautious
about the mushrooms they are inclined to pick. Some are quite
deadly. Nevertheless, he adds that it is impracticable to refrain
altogether from looking for mushrooms, "for even though there
are many things which threaten your existence, you cannot
withdraw your hand from all of them as if you had burned
yourself on them. . . . But, be careful, dear friend. It is not so
easy to see whether they are marked with a cross," the sign
for the dangerous plants in the pickers' guide.[14]

In such a way Borgen counseled resistance even while waiting
for better days. As early as May, 1940, he wrote: Don't be
philosophical, Seize the opportunity when it comes. Do it. Yet
hope and patience were his most fundamental message. He
urges his public to develop "a discipline of waiting," for time
always works in the favor of the waiting person. Occasionally
he despairs for Norway. "A small man, a small land, it never is
a genuine tragedy if they disappear or are killed accidentally"
(August 29, 1941).[15] But the essential tone of the wartime
"mumle gåsegg" reflected hope; and Borgen's active entry into
the Resistance following his imprisonment at Grini illustrated
the chances he was willing to take in order to bring his optimism
in the darkness to fulfillment.

II   Ord gjennom år *and* Alltid på en søndag

After the war Borgen's chief interests turned to his fiction,
and he commenced working on the short stories and novels that

were to establish his literary reputation. Though he failed to take up his regular column in *Dagbladet,* he continued to contribute articles to the newspaper. Moreover, he wrote literary criticism for the periodical *Vinduet* (which he edited from 1954–1959), and he was a frequent cultural commentator on the national radio network. A sampling of Borgen's articles and criticism was published in the volume *Ord gjennom år,* and sixty of the radio talks were printed in *Alltid på en søndag.*

A theme that runs constantly through Borgen's postwar journalism and social commentary is his harsh assessment of the quality of modern life. The war brought out the most savage instincts in man, but it also produced incidents of absolute self-sacrifice. The return to normal seemed to be marked by a surrender to mediocrity. Small problems render us powerless. Borgen skillfully employs the anecdote to make his point. A Swedish couple come to Oslo for a brief visit. They have left their baby with a sitter back home. The plane from Stockholm gets the young couple to the Norwegian capital in fifty minutes; but a petty difficulty, the fact that the Stockholm baby-sitter can work for no more than one day, ruins the couple's stay. They have to rush back home, without having done any of the things they wanted to do. Borgen launches into the welfare state for its preoccupation with power and its insensitivity toward the individual and the weak. Superhighways spread out, but potholes in city streets remain unfilled. Millions are spent on defense, but it is impossible to spend money on decent quarters for retarded children. The welfare state chokes in its bureaucratic red tape and cannot cope with human problems, only technological ones.

Aware that at times he may seem mawkish, Borgen enjoys reveling in a past when problems appeared simpler and approaches to them more direct and wholesome. Occasionally he admits that modern life has a few pleasant surprises, as he discovered on a ski trip that led him one day to a modern logging camp. He found the place comfortable and pleasant, the workers contented and well informed, all of which would have been unheard of in the good old days of his youth.[16] More frequently, however, he considers so-called material progress to be degrading. One morning he observes a neighbor exhausting himself in an attempt to dig his car out of the snow, and in the afternoon he sees the same individual struggling against impossible odds to get his vehicle up a slippery incline. When Borgen suggests that the neighbor abandon his car for the day and walk up the hill, the owner looks at him with a curiously wounded animal expression.[17] Of all the everyday institutions of contemporary life, the supermarket perhaps is the one Borgen detests the most. It has driven Mrs. Johansen into premature retirement and epitomizes the consumer-drugged society. Faceless shelves tempt the shopper to spend his money on items he neither needs nor wants. To add to his confusion food analysts promote and condemn different items—and sometimes the same ones—with regularity. Borgen advises total abandonment of the experts and proposes "COMMON SENSE. A LITTLE OF EACH KIND. And an arrow pointing to the roomiest of all health stations: NATURE."[18]

To Borgen the busy character of modern life contributes to the inefficiency of modern labor. Nothing truly gets accomplished, no one truly experiences anything. The five-day tourist in Spain may well be the most appropriate symbol of the contemporary world, exhausted, on a treadmill of fleeting impulses, numbed. In place of Costa del Sol or Mallorca, Borgen proposes a fishing trip in a nearby fjord, or a bicycle ride through the city and beyond it. What are living moments of genuine, remembered quality? A sunrise, the perfume of fields in the early morning, the spectacular play of light on a mountain in Finnmark. Such are the invaluable pauses in the routine of modern life, providing the moods for introspection that Borgen's fictional characters will be hunting for.

Modern society lacks honesty and expects none from its institutions and leaders. No one expects an insurance company to fulfill its side of a contract, no one expects a politician to abide by campaign promises. Moral courage is meaningless. A driver flees the scene of an accident he has caused, a witness to a crime prefers to disappear rather than risk involvement. We read about racial injustice in Rhodesia, political repression in Greece, war atrocities in Vietnam, and then turn to the television previews which, of course, are intended to lull us. In a particularly bitter piece, written in 1966, Borgen heaps scorn upon the leadership of the Norwegian Labor Party for advising members to refrain from joining the Vietnam Solidarity Committee.[19] Borgen the denunciator of capitalism shares a place with Borgen the ascetic individualist. The consumer society encourages greed; greed inevitably leads to war: Borgen's popular journalism, from the 1920's to the 1970's, is an attempt to awaken his audience to this point. Merely hoping for a livable world is not enough; but Borgen believes that we still have reason to hope, "as long as we all realize that it is in the power of man—and absolutely not that of any god—to transform hope into reality."[20]

III *Borgen's Literary Criticism*

Literary criticism forms a significant part of Borgen's contribution to journalism. Far removed from the academic variety, it is a spontaneous, personal kind of criticism. Borgen often discovers in other authors themes similar to those expressed in his own writings. His opinions on the function of the critic are close to Baudelaire's; and in an article dealing with Paul la Cour's Danish edition of Baudelaire's esthetics, Borgen quotes the French poet: "I am convinced that the best type of criticism is the lively and poetic, not the cool, mathematical kind that pretends to explain everything in order to mask its inability to be passionately for or against anything, and which freely abstains from expressing any sort of emotion."[21]

Borgen agrees with Baudelaire that criticism should be passionate. Its essential function is to illustrate the reaction of an intelligent, sensitive mind to an individual work of art. This is as broad a definition as Borgen can find, for the critic must be permitted as much leeway of expression as the artist himself. Criticism must not try to fit a work of art into a formula or system. Such an effort is doomed to failure anyway. Nor should the critic tamper with the artist's language in order to make him more readily understandable. In short, Borgen's criticism is that of a fellow-writer, and he believes that an artist makes the exemplary critic. His models for criticism are Baudelaire's essays on Delacroix and Poe.

To Borgen the overriding purpose of criticism is to keep the spirit of a work alive and to elucidate effectively the artist's intentions. Therefore Borgen is very sympathetic toward attempts at transforming literary pieces into visual art. In an article that compared Orson Welles's motion picture version of Kafka's *The Trial* with a version that appeared over Norwegian television, Borgen found the latter to be extremely effective. In remaining true to Kafka's mood and message, the television play did the novel an enormous service. In the sense of clarity and universality it even surpassed the novel. To those who might call this viewpoint sacrilegious or even nonsense, Borgen responds unequivocally "that there are only a few who can read, but many who can see."[22] On a single evening tens of thousands of Norwegians, who might have missed the point of *The Trial* had they attempted to read the novel, were able to grasp its significance. Borgen has always been attracted to the visual arts. In *Barndommens rike* he states that painting is more important to him than literature.[23]

Since Borgen the critic so deeply desires a passionate experience with a work of art, his articles on other novelists provide valuable guides to his own fiction. The themes he analyzes in other writers are the ones he explores with most interest in his novels and short stories—social alienation, the quests for identity and innocence, the artist's search for congruence between meaning and form. The stories of the Belgian novelist Georges Simenon particularly attract him. Simenon's heroes often have lost their ability to stop and take stock of their lives. For example, Simenon's novel *The Heart of a Man* is, according to Borgen, a penetrating study of "a richly endowed human mind that never took time out for meditation, that never had the courage to dig into itself, that never located the surplus to sink ever so little."[24] The actor Mauguin's failure to come to terms with his own past leads him into alcoholism, and only at the conclusion of his life does he begin to look for the root of his problems, the place "where he started to go astray and become the author of evil." Fumbling around his place of origin, Mauguin never reaches his goal: "The clever Simenon surely is no guide through No-man's Land—and thank heaven for that. But in the mental jungle of contrasting impulses he is a searcher of rare quality."[25]

In his own work Borgen lays stress upon pursuit rather than attainment. In this he finds an affinity with Hemingway, whose work is highly important to him. During a radio talk in 1958, Borgen stated his interpretation of Hemingway's life and career. Borgen found that, despite the general personal success Hemingway had achieved in his lifetime, the authentic part of the writer had nothing in common with the mythologized side. Rather than the extoller of masculine virtues, Borgen's Hemingway is: "The individual wounded early. And the one who, in all humility, never tires of educating himself. In spite of his external riches. In spite of his obvious success."[26] To illustrate his point Borgen refers to the hero of one of Hemingway's minor novels, written in the period of his so-called decline. The character is Harry Morgan, of *To Have and Have Not*. The unsuccessful life of the externally successful Harry rings out like a scream. Until he receives a bullet in the stomach, Harry exists without truly having lived. When he realizes that his wound is fatal, he undertakes his clumsy quest for identity. And he never manages to resolve it.

For Borgen, Harry's cry is Hemingway's. Hemingway is a wounded seeker who represents his quest for identity in art. His work betrays a desperate struggle to express his emotions through accurately descriptive words. Of course, *The Old Man and the Sea* was Hemingway's most vivid and logical representation of his quest. But the theme suffuses all of his work: "In our rereading of his great works, we always encounter Hemingway the seeker. The seeker is the artist. Before his work the artist is lonely and small—a dwarf confronting his task which always grows and grows."[27] Harry Morgan never resolves his identity crisis, and Hemingway never obtained the perfect congruence he was after between meaning and form. Each work of art was the fruit of a painful, introspective moment, analogous to the moment when Harry received his bullet wound. Borgen underscores the artist's pain: "How many bullets in the stomach must the artist receive? How often, like Harry Morgan, must he believe he is bleeding to death before the brief, blissful instants arrive when he at least can *pretend* that there is congruence between intention and expression—?"[28]

For Borgen, as for Hemingway, creativity is linked up with

awareness of death. Death may justifiably preoccupy the writer. Borgen takes to task "superficial" critics who pejoratively called Hemingway a death-worshiper: "Personally, I think it is more appropriate to see [in his intention] a kind of obsessive worship of life."[29] This must be so because for the authentic writer such as Hemingway the moments of painful introspection are the only ones during which the artist considers himself to be living genuinely.

No single novel has had a more profound effect upon Borgen than Knut Hamsun's *Mysteries*. The novel describes the thirty-five days preceding the suicide of the protagonist Nagel. It is during this period that Nagel attempts, and fails, to create an identity. Borgen's fascination with *Mysteries* is intimately related to his fascination with the novel's author. Borgen finds that, during the period of the novel's composition, Hamsun's correspondence rings out like "a cry from a soul in need."[30]

Nagel is a hypersensitive individual who has learned to hide his excessive vulnerability behind a mask of scornful defiance. He desperately tries to dispense with his mask and establish an authentic kind of existence. On failing, he commits suicide. According to Borgen, the creation of Nagel had a profound effect upon Hamsun's own personality. It made him aware of a side of himself hitherto suppressed almost beyond recognition. After completing *Mysteries*, Hamsun was to hold up a mask of contempt for most others that became notorious, and it culminated in his degradation as a Nazi collaborator during World War II. "One does not write [a novel like] *Mysteries* without being damaged by it. And the damage enriches the poet, even though it may cost him—yes, all human decency."[31] The novelist's discovery of the affinity with his hero is a problem that disturbs Borgen. He may well have feared that, through his own art, he would find a side of himself similar to what Hamsun discovered through his creation of Nagel.

For Borgen a work of art is a confession. The writer succeeds in direct proportion to his willingness and skill at exposing his inner life.[32] Hamsun at least possessed the courage to bare his self ruthlessly. So did another writer whom Borgen admires, the Dane H. C. Branner. In an address to the students at the University of Oslo, Borgen analyzed Branner's short story

"Bjergene" ("The Mountains"): "When I first read 'Bjergene,' I became frightened. I believed that no one could survive a confession like that."[33] The protagonist of Branner's story is a poet with an absurd-sounding name, Claus Klumpe. Claus is Branner's foil for displaying sides of the author's personality that shame him. To illustrate the point, Borgen refers to Ibsen's definition of the poet as both judge and accused.[34] In "Bjergene" Branner accuses the poet of manipulating human suffering for artistic ends. Borgen sees this as Branner's self-accusation. The Dane severely questions his own calling, one that thrives upon genuine suffering in order to obtain material for fantasy and dream. Branner asks, and Borgen reiterates, the question: Is the poet playing life instead of living it? Is he searching for a crutch that will enable him to escape responsibility?

Claus's girl friend is his *alter ego*. She notes that Claus "was not faithful to anything or anyone. At any moment he could take leave of places and people as though they never had existed."[35] In Borgen's own work, there exists a genuine conflict between the dreaming poet and the female who has accepted the responsibilities of life. In his discussion of Branner, Borgen suggests that the male and the female character may represent the two sides of the poet himself. The female voice exposes the guilt that the artist feels for having sacrificed the reality of the world for dream. The work of art, the writer's confession, is the consequence of a ruthless self-examination. Therefore, it provides the artist with a legitimate, though temporary, release from guilt. One time finished, the process must begin anew. As Borgen puts it, "It represents a new cross-examination, new poetry, new and endless scratchings in the crater, so that it may vomit forth fires of beauty—once more, once more."[36]

CHAPTER 3

On Imagination and Art

I *The Return to Childhood*

IN all of Borgen's work childhood occupies a privileged place. It is frequently associated with lazy summer days by the sea and represents a spot to which all adult characters long to return. It is their paradise lost, an Eden from which they were exiled long ago.

Borgen begins his essay *Innbilningen og kunsten* with the tale of an elderly executive who, toward the end of his career, lost interest in his work and absorbed himself in the childhood memory of a beetle crawling upon a piece of straw.[1] The old man's relatives began suspecting him of senility and, appropriately enough, anticipated their inheritance. Borgen, however, associates his hero's preoccupation with the discovery of having forgotten the nature of his genuine personality. The old executive's busy life had made it necessary for him to conform his personality with his role in society. In turn his role imposed limits upon his behavior and thoughts. Since the role required him to occupy himself with hundreds of daily details, his memory became stunted and he was the slave of secretaries and notes. In the midst of material success the businessman became a pitiful figure. He lost all contact with his authentic self. His social obligations formed a cage around him, preventing his development as a full, human being.

Borgen sees an analogy between his executive and Peer Gynt. For many years the businessman remained confident that his passport was sufficient evidence of his identity. One day, however, some overzealous border guards scrutinized the document more closely, comparing the photograph in it with the face of its bearer. They concluded that the person before them no longer resembled the picture, and they refused him permission to cross the frontier.[2] Borgen sees Peer Gynt's encounter with the button-maker—to him the climax of Ibsen's play—in terms similar to his executive's misadventure with the border guards. The button-maker considers Peer to be a useless button and is anxious to throw him into the melting pot in order to free him for more profitable use.[3] Likewise, the border guards question the personality assumed by Borgen's businessman and would just as well discard it as unauthentic. The border guards, like the button-maker, are intrusions of a guilty conscience. Peer and the executive had spent most of their adult lives wasting whatever potential they had possessed. Never once had they reached into their true selves to establish their authenticity. Never once had they taken time out for the contemplative pauses necessary for self-examination and the possibility of self-awareness.[4] After his frightening encounter with the button-maker Peer of course does reevaluate his existence, and is saved through the intervention of the faithful Solveig, whose purity of heart always had kept her authentic. And following his encounter with the guards Borgen's executive reestablishes a line of communication with his genuine self by withdrawing from his life of activity and returning to the childlike pleasure of contemplating the beetle on the straw. Like a prisoner who discovers his cage to have miraculously collapsed, he is liberated sufficiently to experience profound happiness. His return to childhood legitimizes fantasy for him. He becomes receptive to the mystique of nature. He crosses the border of Reason and reenters the golden land of imagination and dream which he had left years earlier during the transition from childhood to adolescence.

For Borgen the return to childhood is not necessarily an end in itself. Rather, it represents a way station that permits an individual to reestablish contact with the source from which all human beings derive. One's eligibility for returning to this source depends upon one's escape from the cage of Reason. Borgen calls the source the "ur-jeg" ("original I") and he singles out Dostoevski as a writer who was primarily concerned with searching his way back to it.[5] The quest for the original self offers a mystical quality to some of Borgen's work. The search for childhood is identified both with the quest for individual authenticity and cosmic union. When he peered at the photograph in

his passport, the old executive painfully understood that his true
self had disappeared. When he contemplated the beetle on the
straw, he rediscovered his roots and at the same moment obtained
a sense of universal awareness: "What was he then?" he asked.
"A child. All."[6] Ultimately the quest for identity, so crucial in
Borgen's work, is not essentially a quest for singularity of
consciousness. It is a search for cosmic union.

II *The Role of Art*

For Borgen, the artist is a privileged being. Through his work
the artist may reestablish contact with the lost self. He is successful in proportion to his ability to give verbal or visual
expression to his quest. Since essentially it represents the quest
for a truer reality, art never can be merely the imitation of
external reality. It is an error to accuse the artist of failing
to conform to the laws of Reason. On the contrary, Reason is
a barrier through which the artist must crash if he will be true
to his vocation. In looking for the source he must cross indefin-
able frontiers. The essence of genuine art must be experimental.
In his novels from *Lillelord* through *Min arm, min tarm* Borgen
will make attempts to test out this hypothesis.

The artist, according to Borgen, is not necessarily unique in
his longing. But the artist is less willing than others to repress
his desire to recapture his lost identity. Modern life forces us
to sublimate in a thousand ways our need to reach the source
of the self. Our work and distractions lead us away from the
essential. The communications media fill our lives with fragments
of events we never shall be able to explore in depth. The technological miracles of our age turn us away from the experience
of deeply felt emotions and make introspection virtually impossible. Physically and mentally exhausted, modern man has
little strength left for pursuing what ought to represent his
primary goal.

It therefore is the artist's mission to counter our distractions
and reverse the process that has alienated man from his genuine
identity. The purpose of art is twofold. It liberates the artist
and can liberate an audience receptive to his message. The
ultimate identity for which the artist is searching is not his alone,

but one that is common to all human beings. Therefore, the work of art will help the receptive viewer or reader to advance more readily in his own quest. In *Innbilningens verden* Borgen awards to art the mission of bringing the reader into contact with essences that elude him in his daily routine. Art must help break down the barriers that each individual constructs around the self. It must assist the individual in returning to the universal source of being.

Borgen does not believe that the trained specialist possesses a monopoly of communicability with the artist. On the contrary, the contact between audience and artist must be based upon emotions, never upon the intellect. The receptive moment is spontaneous and inexplicable. The viewer or reader is shaken from his habitual, lethargic existence and in a flash perceives the path he must follow if he is to recover his lost identity. Borgen is certain that great numbers of people are at least vaguely aware of the true function of art and are searching for the liberating experience that will set them loose from their routine selves. As evidence, he conjures up the image of crowds wandering about art galleries throughout the world, in search of beauty and perhaps subconsciously the manner in which beauty may transform their lives.

III *Brainwash*

In a section of *Innbilningens verden* Borgen reveals his fascination with the practice of brainwashing prisoners of war, so that their conventional personalities break down. Borgen refrains from dealing with the moral question raised by such practice, and rather notes the relative ease with which the trained washer achieves his results. Simply and quickly he can destroy a personality and construct a wholly different one in its place. By isolating the prisoner for a certain period of time and exposing him to a certain set of stimuli, one can make the victim forget his telephone number, the names of his spouse and children, even his own name. Thus the prisoner's former social personality is erased, and he is completely unable to identify himself. A personality with so little power of resistance, reasons Borgen, is exceedingly fragile. It is a bomb shelter whose walls

offer merely the illusion of protection. Put to the first serious
test, the walls collapse.

According to Borgen, man's unhappiness in the modern world
stems from a refusal to come to terms with his true self. Nevertheless, people are aware of the unauthenticity of their social
personalities. They feel guilt over this; and this theme, according
to Borgen, is central to modern art and literature. Though they
interpreted the complex of guilt differently, both Dostoevski
and Kafka exploited it in their work. For Dostoevski guilt had
its source not within society but as a consequence of original
sin, and liberation was the equivalent of a religious awakening.
For Kafka guilt develops as the individual draws himself more
deeply into the social whirl. The arrival of the accusers represents the awakening of Joseph K.'s conscience. The refusal of
the accusers to accept Joseph K.'s identity papers corresponds
to the border guards' rejection of the passport of Borgen's
executive. Once he no longer can accept his unauthentic existence, Joseph K. is unable to return to his job as a bank clerk.
The volume of psychic evidence accumulates and turns his
total existence into a nightmare. He is unable to confess his
guilt, but ultimately accepts it and his punishment. To the
twentieth-century reader, Joseph K. represents Everyman. The
guilt that suffuses *The Trial* is universally shared. It fosters
angst, and in fact is the basis for the entire *angst* motif in modern
literature. Our hell stems from the unauthenticity of our selves,
not from our supposed universal fear of the Bomb.[7]

In Borgen's view modern man needs a thorough brainwash in
order to liberate himself from his unauthentic social personality
and relieve himself of his guilt. We all need a moment of total
revelation that will permit us to contemplate our beetles on
the straw. And it is the function of art to help us attain our
privileged moment. This is the clear and simple message of
Innbilningens verden. The essay is an essential starting point
for an analysis of Johan Borgen's literary production. Once they
become aware of their loss of identity, once they realize that
they are mere puppets lost in a social whirl, all of Borgen's
heroes experience their crisis of consciousness. They find themselves in a spiritual wasteland that is transformed into a physical
one. Customarily, it is a deserted, unfriendly landscape not far

from the frontier over which they wish to escape. Borgen uses the term Nobiskro to describe the wasteland that represents our barren spiritual life.[8] The individual aware of Nobiskro no longer can accept his old life. In wishing to rid himself of it he becomes asocial, restless, and may resort to criminal acts. He resembles a caged animal, pacing around in search of an exit. While he may not comprehend very clearly the reasons lurking behind his restlessness, he longs for a path toward liberation. He believes that the first way station toward liberation is the return to childhood. Here the Borgen hero hopes to locate spiritual authenticity. But childhood is only a way station, and it is of course unattainable. Just as unattainable is the original self that lies beyond childhood.

When he writes about the attainment of true liberty, or genuine reconciliation with the original self, Borgen becomes ambiguous and skeptical. There are times when he leads us to believe that the quest is futile. Art may help an individual break down his social personality and reestablish lines of communication between him and his authentic self; it may lead the individual to the border of total human experience. But when all is said and done, the artist is no more than another human being. He cannot will himself across the frontier; he cannot take the reader across. The genuine crossing, the return to the universal self, can be attained only through death. As Borgen's heroes achieve their goal, their author is forced to abandon them. The characters escape even their creator, who is left with a corpse. Thus the artist may indicate the path leading to "the place," but it is beyond his power to reveal its secret. The essential purpose of art, then, is to communicate the artist's longing for the boundless and awaken a similar longing in others.

Innbilningens verden was published in 1960, after the *Lillelord* trilogy, *"Jeg,"* and Borgen's most important short stories. The fiction is not meant merely to illustrate the theories Borgen summarized in his essay. On the contrary, the fiction represents Borgen's confession of his struggle with certain fundamental problems of life, art, and death. The characters who are most successful in their quests find no simple answers. Rather, they often discover that along with losing touch with daily routine they have lost touch with other human beings. Instead of finding their emotional receptivity stimulated, they find themselves oriented exclusively toward the past and toward death. Borgen seems to regret this deeply, and often wonders whether it is at all possible to return to authenticity without at the same time denying life. This is an agonizing problem in all his novels from *Lillelord* through *Min arm, min tarm,* as well as in many of the short stories. One of Borgen's most persistent themes is the conflict between the quest and human love. The life-accepting characters of course are not bloodless social conformists. They are privileged individuals who have escaped an identity crisis and have kept the channel to childhood open. Their very simplicity prevents them from comprehending their more complicated partners whom they will either abandon or pull back from the quest. It is the presence of these characters—perhaps an *alter ego* beating in the breast of the artist himself—that identifies Borgen as a writer who questions more effectively than he answers.

CHAPTER 4

Dream and Reality in the Short Stories

LONG before he acquired celebrity as a novelist, Borgen was known as an accomplished short-story writer. His most important early stories appeared in four collections: *Barnesinn* (1937); *Hvetebrødsdager* (1948); *Noveller om kjærlighet* (1952); *Natt og dag* (1954). In 1961 the Oslo publishing house Gyldendal came out with a collection of new and previously published stories, *Noveller i utvalg 1936–1961*; in 1965 a new collection appeared, *Nye noveller*; and in 1969, Borgen published his latest contributions, *Trær alene i skogen*. Since the stories in the latter collection differ from the others in theme and tone I have chosen to discuss them in a subsequent chapter.

The subject matter of Borgen's stories varies: several underscore his concern for recapturing a simpler, primitive life style; others have to do with the longing for innocence and childhood; a few use the war as a central theme. In the main, the major ideas that Borgen places into his novels are also his concerns in the short stories—that is, the problem of identity, the crisis of consciousness, awareness of death.

I *The Quest for Identity*

Borgen's most significant short stories concern the quest for identity. A crisis of consciousness customarily jolts the character out of his diurnal existence, and he comes to realize his insignificance within the universal order. Far from provoking fear alone, the awareness of death instills in the character an irresistible longing to reunite with the cosmos, the presence of which he feels with overwhelming intensity. The character undergoing crisis becomes restless to the point of "dropping out." He forsakes society and the child within him revives. These symptoms appear either simultaneously or consecutively;

49

but they always serve to identify the individual searching for the source of the self. A wish to cross a vaguely defined frontier, climb a tower or a mountain peak, or sink into a body of water illustrates the hero's obsession to be absorbed in an absolute.[1]

The only emotion powerful and authentic enough to challenge the "boundless longing" is love. In Borgen's work love always represents a strongly positive, life-affirming force. This is especially true in the short stories, where love is identical with passion. It is built upon the spontaneous experience of communication between a man and a woman. Because it provides the individual with the opportunity to drop his social mask and express genuine emotions, the experience of love is closely related to that of childhood and far removed from that of society. Nevertheless, most often love cannot satisfy the individual's thirst for identity. On the contrary, while the character in quest of identity and the character in quest of love customarily are attracted to one another, the relationship between the two is very difficult. By its nature the quest for identity is "boundless," based upon a desire to drive through all barriers, and concluding with the dissolution of the ego. The sex act concludes with a similar experience, but only for a fleeting moment. The difficulty arises when the couple attempt to prolong their love in a more lasting union. Mutual devotion permits a man and woman to escape the cage of society, but the two construct yet a more lasting cage around one another. In the long run love and the quest for identity must come into conflict. For a time the yearning hero may welcome love as a means toward liberation, but often he reaches the point of rejecting it if he is to continue his quest. While he slips into his dreams of childhood, the beloved is left with a feeling of betrayal and will try to prevent his escape. A struggle ensues. The beloved will consider it a duty to rescue the lover. In Borgen's short stories this duality between love and longing forms a pervasive theme. Since the dreamer may be either male or female, Borgen does not resort to sexual stereotypes. Observing his entire literary production, however, one notices a pronounced shift toward the idea of the yearning male and the life-affirming female. In the novels such a distribution becomes consistent.

II *The Crisis of Consciousness*

In "Kaprifolium" ("Honeysuckle Vine") and "Natt og dag 1" ("Night and Day 1") the protagonist is a young boy. Since the central character is too young for adult, erotic love, the family group represents the life-affirming forces. In the first story the boy has an irresistible urge to climb a honeysuckle vine that decorates one of the walls of the house where he lives with his family. His parents declare the plant off limits, but the fragrance of the flowers draws him on. Climbing the vine one day, the boy becomes overwhelmed by the aroma. He is caught in the branches and loses consciousness. The parents find and rescue him, and then bring him into the house. As he slowly revives, the boy feels a desperate sensation of loneliness.

"Kaprifolium" has strong, mystical overtones. The parents of the boy stand for safety within the framework of normal, daily life. In contrast, the flowers represent the temptation of a prohibited world where the self dissolves into the universe. As the boy climbs the vine, Borgen likens him to a fish caught in a net: "The fragrance of honeysuckle has numbed him, so that reality drifts away and becomes quite distant. He does not even feel 'danger' now. No, it is the net he has stepped into, the honeysuckle net which had been set to catch him. And he is never to be released from his metamorphosis."[2] As a sudden rainstorm descends upon the boy, the fish image gains in impact. The vine assumes the shape of a cross, literally impaling the boy in its branches. Locked in the net of the arbor he loses consciousness and senses a momentary extinction of the self. He becomes a humanized Christ. Gradually the feeling of forsakenness transforms into one of universal union: "All. Beyond the yoke of his exhaustion this is what he senses. He is no longer a honeysuckle. Not a fish. He is *all*. He possesses everybody's knowledge of the boundless and of his own helplessness. He feels this new experience as a confirmation of what he always must have known: first a dizzy pleasure on the frontier of bodily anguish; then a spiritual loneliness without limits."[3] As the boy looks into the evening sky, two stars stare back at him in piercing fashion: "In that moment he begins to know something about man's precarious position within a whole."[4]

Since all human beings share the same cosmic fate, the transformation of the individual into all affirms the idea of universal
solidarity. The magnetic attraction the boy feels toward the
vine reflects his need to escape from the prison of the self.
It is his death wish. The boy's yearning is so powerful that he
undergoes a series of metamorphoses and loses consciousness.
He becomes a fish, then part of the vine, finally a crucified
Christ. The imagery strongly suggests the sacrifice of the individual self as a necessary step toward cosmic union. Abruptly
torn away from the vine by his horrified parents, the boy finds
his trance broken. Almost instantaneously his expanded self
deflates, and he again is no more than a boy in bed. Nevertheless, the experience will permanently mark him with the stamp
of loneliness. He becomes the prototype of the later Borgen
hero torn between the rival forces of isolation and society, dream
and reality, death and life.

The theme of "Natt og dag 1" is similar to that of "Kaprifolium." On an August evening a young boy hidden in the
garden of his parents' house overhears the conversation of
adults. While members of the group speak, they behold the
circling of several bats above their heads. To the boy, invisible
forces seem to be steering the bats clear of impediments. The
eavesdropper overhears disconnected parts of sentences. The
words "mortal danger" and "longing" ring in his ears. As an
impulse to be absorbed in the darkness seizes the boy, the words
assume personal significance. Above his head the stars form a
glittering net, tempting him to abandon the self to the infinity
that envelops him. Unlike the bats, the boy does not have a
built-in radar protecting him from danger. He does not seek the
safety of the garden but is attracted to the distant light of the
stars. Instinctively he begins to move toward the sea that lies
just beyond the garden. Only when he touches the water and
starts drifting with the current does he appreciate the danger.
The glare from a distant lighthouse awakens him. He swims
toward it and reaches safety on a promontory near the beacon.

Unlike the protagonist in "Kaprifolium," the boy in "Natt og
dag 1" has chosen life over dissolution. In the end the man-made
beacon proved to be a more powerful attraction to him than
the stars in the summer sky. Yet the experience of the tempta-

tion will mark him all his life. Words he hears will carry more than just their surface meaning. His brush with death will provide him with an object lesson—an expanded sensitivity toward existence: "Barefoot he went across the rocks, passed the inlet containing the lighthouse keeper's boat, and entered a sheltered leafy forest. He walked fast and softly and dreaded nothing. For the first time he had the night behind him, but still he felt it within. It would always be within him, for he knew something about the relationship between things."[5] The boy's reaction to his experience brings to mind the attitude of Camus's Sisyphus, who continued to roll his rock in full awareness of the futility of the task. Unlike Camus's hero, however, the enrichment that Borgen's boy will find takes the form of a serene loneliness, not a life of humanitarian action.

The familiar Borgen theme of a crisis of consciousness is central to two other stories, "En klar dag i mai" ("A Clear Day in May") and "Forandringen" ("Change"). In the first story Old Bino has been blind since his youth. During a total eclipse of the sun the population of the small town where he lives experiences his perpetual darkness. The darkness has a clearly existential significance. It represents awareness of a sunless, lifeless universe: "The people stood silent feeling the heavenly bodies sail by and they noticed that they themselves were a sailing part of a whole, that they were in space, that they were a part of space, and that space and they were linked in a powerless union, and it was as if a cold distrust spread from person to person, though they were not looking at one another and they knew that no one could help anyone, with anything."[6] For no more than an instant the townspeople share Bino's loneliness. Once the sun reappears all but a single couple return to their daily routine. This young man and woman, who prior to the eclipse had been absorbed in their own happiness, discover a wedge between them: "A short while ago they had run across the fields together, they had not even known that there was supposed to be an eclipse. They had not known anything. They had been happy. Now they stood there alone in the town square, and they stood close to one another but he could not reach her."[7] Unmarked by the eclipse, the young man seems willing to return to his customary life. But his beloved comprehends how near she had been to total solitude and dissolution. For her, nothing will ever be the same again. Noticing the change in his fiancée, the man observes Old Bino: "'Now I understand,' he said quietly. 'You are thinking that he always has it that way. It must be terrible,' he said. She did not look up. 'It is not terrible,' she said."[8] The young woman has discovered the serene pleasure of awareness and therefore refuses to compromise her newly acquired sensitivity with the realities of daily existence.

Included in Borgen's collection *Nye noveller*, the story "Forandringen" ("Change") is constructed upon a foundation of contrasts. These are noise and silence, storm and calm, change and eternity, life and death. One day a man is wrenched from his routine when he discovers that the noise around him has been transformed into total silence. Furthermore, for a fraction of a second all objects become immobilized. People turn into statues. The experience affects him personally, and from this moment on simple objects take on a sinister, allusive quality. The light that penetrates his room at dawn becomes a spear; his diver's mask on the wall converts into a death mask staring down at him. The protagonist has a nightmare in which he sinks into the sea and disappears. What he seemingly learns from his experience is that while life is identical with flux, all living things tend irrevocably toward immobility. He is part of the inevitable process, and his every action awakes in him the sensation of dying. He touches a tree and senses it change: "He touches the tree trunk as he passes it, and feels that it is cold and rough. But the tree changes under his hand, grows, nourishes itself, ages. The tree is a process, like himself, like all living things, things that soon will die."[9]

A scene in Sartre's *La Nausée* offers an illuminating contrast with the incident of the protagonist and the tree in "Forandringen." In the city park Roquentin observes the growth of a tree root. He becomes overwhelmed with nausea. He is unable to tolerate the existence of any living thing devoid of consciousness. On the other hand, awareness of a union of existence between his self and the tree inspires Borgen's hero. He longs to melt into the universe. Awareness of death does not transform him into a rebel, but rather lifts him out of his ordinary existence into a world of peace and serenity: "But everyone noticed the man's calm, it gave them pleasure. . . . They saw him lift his hands, folded; he resembled a church as he stood there against the sea which was white and wild with foam."[10] The experience is not, as it may first seem, a Christian one. It appears closer to the Buddhist notion that man can attain serenity by contemplating his own dissolution.

III   *Love and Longing*

On several occasions Borgen pursues the theme of love as an obstacle in the quest for the source of the self. Love prevents the Borgen hero from becoming absorbed in his world of contemplation and fantasy. In "Kaprifolium" it was parental love that snatched the boy from the vine and restored him to his bed in the house. In "En klar dag i mai" the fiancé struggled to no avail against the influence of the eclipse upon his beloved. In the story "Moses," a sequel to "Forandringen," the widow of a dreamer equates love with familial obligation. Her deceased husband had withdrawn into himself. Now she accuses him of having engaged in psychological self-indulgence that destroyed the family's well-being. Her complaints veil a lack of comprehension that merits little sympathy from the reader. In "Victoria Regia" Borgen constructs the preface of a male-female relationship that will pit dream against reality. By chance a couple meet in a botanical garden and strike up a conversation. The man relishes his fantasy existence and longs to preserve his links to childhood. The woman, caught up in society, suppresses her emotions and worries about her physical appearance. Gradually, in the humid hothouse, the woman succumbs to the influence of her companion, and the protective walls she has built around herself peel away. Sensing her mask slip, she fumbles for a mirror as if to reassure herself that she is the same person who entered the garden. She cannot find the mirror, nor can she summon the will to leave the garden by herself. Ultimately she and the man walk out together. Her companion has challenged her existence and overwhelmed it. Here Borgen ends the story. He offers no hint as to the permanence of the dreamer's victory. Nor does he suggest whether the couple's budding love can develop and grow in this atmosphere.

In another story, "Fuglen og fristeren" ("The Bird and the Tempter"), the intervention of love into the universe of the dreamer terminates in disaster. A woman, Gro, tires of her dull, middle-class life, and leaves her husband. She takes a dreamer, Fartein, as her lover and prepares to accept his universe as the basis for their union. The two experience a short, hectic love affair, exempted from the rules of behavior by which ordinary people must abide. Fartein and Gro think of their love almost as a religious ecstasy, and they know that they will never again be able to return to a normal, social existence. At the end Fartein commits suicide. Deranged with grief, Gro is committed to a mental hospital, where she tries to evoke in dream her erstwhile ecstasy. Her husband pleads with her to return to him, but she consciously prefers isolation until death. To the outside world she is insane. Borgen seems to sympathize with her withdrawal from daily reality, but he also underscores how her passion upset the dreamer's delicate balance, ultimately destroying both Fartein and herself.

In three other stories Borgen explores the consequences when a life-oriented female tries to pull her lover from his reverie. In "Hun ville det" ("She Willed It") five men have abandoned themselves to a drinking party that lasts far into the night. Early the next morning they decide to go to a neighborhood café for breakfast. The café is located in the town square, which the group can reach by passing through a narrow street lined with sixteenth-century buildings. As the men leave the house and begin walking down the street, their brief journey is transformed into a nightmare. Before their eyes the passage narrows, the buildings close in on one another. Between the mass of stone the sky all but disappears. The men are seized with panic. They try to return to the place from which they started, only to discover that their route has closed behind them. As the men lose hope of surviving, the narrator sets his attention upon one of the buildings. Fixed to it is a sculptured medallion representing a woman in heraldic dress. Suddenly the woman springs to life, spreads out a pair of powerful wings, and with her body begins to push apart the buildings that threaten to crush the frantic men. At last she provides an opening toward the sky and the square. "Onward!" the narrator shouts to his frightened friends.

"She wills it!" What the woman wishes, of course, is to save the men. They start running and reach the café in the square. Unlike his companions, the narrator harbors some regrets about leaving the passage. Following behind his friends and emerging into the light, he senses powerful forces drawing him back toward the sinister alley, now a dull mass of stone.

The symbolism in "Hun ville det" is built upon fantasy. Still, it recalls familiar Borgen themes. In their drinking party the men forsook their routine existence for a world of illusion and dream. The café represents the restoration of their customary life, but they find it more difficult and dangerous to return than they had imagined. Dissolution, symbolized by the dark alley and its sinister buildings, threatens to engulf them. What saves them, however, is the eternal representation of woman. She extricates them from the threat of death and restores them to their routine cares and joys. As the story's title suggests, it is through sheer willpower that the woman finds the necessary strength to push apart the masses of stone. She is, in fact, the men's guardian angel, standing perhaps for the wives they have left behind.[11]

"Hun ville det" offers a pattern of sexual roles that Borgen adheres to in his novels, though he is less consistent about it in his short stories. The male is the dreamer, the female the realist. The woman proposes the alternative to death, a ray of daylight stemming from human love. Nevertheless, once having tasted the temptation of the night, the male remains restless. However dangerous that world may have been, a desire to return to it will never leave him. Though the parents in "Kaprifolium" and the woman in "Hun ville det" restore the hero to safety, his exposure to the danger leaves its mark. He feels an urge to find it again.

In "Stjernen" ("The Star"), the most poignant love story in *Noveller i utvalg*, Borgen introduces a variation on his male-female theme. A young man brings his girl to a place by the sea where he used to spend his childhood. It is the Eden about which he often has spoken to her, and he does not tire of asking her whether it is as she had imagined it from his descriptions. The girl finds herself absorbed in his dream world. As the pair make love in a sheltered spot called Paradise, she senses the dissolution of her ego. Afterwards the young man reverts to his familiar pastime of telling stories about his childhood. He relates one about a party in the family's summer house. The party was to conclude with a fireworks display, and for the first time the ten-year-old boy would be permitted to shoot off a flare of his own. When the flare turned out to be a dud, his disappointment crushed him. To calm her son the mother then pointed to a barely visible, distant star just appearing in the evening sky. She said: "There is your flare! It flew up there and became a star...."[12] The young man confesses to his beloved that until her arrival his life had been a drab night. But she is the isolated star that now brightens it. This saddens the girl, who comprehends that her lover's affection, like the basis for his mother's explanation, is built upon an illusion. She considers her lover's obsessive withdrawal into childhood fantasy to be an escape from the reality she accepts. He does not desire a companion willing to share with him the problems of life. On the contrary, he is looking for one who will listen to his recollections and be drawn into the universe of his imagination. The girl feels defeated. She rejects the unreal beauty of the landscape, the sea endlessly breaking against the shore, the house haunted by memories of her lover's childhood. Later she withdraws from the house where he lies sleeping:

She was frightened and he did not help her. He slept. She went quickly towards the door, ran.

And when she got outside and felt the path beneath her, she continued to run and in the lightning she saw the path before her. She did not run back to the place from where they had come [the sea], but continued inland, towards trees and familiar things and away from the waves which would engulf her and creep into her and transform her into seaweeds rooted in the surf.

She did not turn around to look at the sea and the house which stood heavily in the night behind her. She ran. Branches struck her face and hands, she liked it, for it was familiar and firm and not soft as silken grass in a sultry breeze.

She ran away from longing, from the ocean and from *him*, and from the dream of returning to childhood.[13]

The girl's fears are related to her lover's penchant for dream. The vocabulary in the passage reflects a fear of losing hold of herself and being absorbed into a soft, tempting element (the waves, the silken grass, the darkness, and her lover's dream). She therefore welcomes the hardness of the path, the bright flashes of lightning, and the concrete pain caused by the branches whipping against her body. She parts from her lover's world, with its associations of the dissolving self, death embodied in the sea, and the temptation for the individual to drown in its eternal perfection.

Whereas "Stjernen" ends with the separation of the lovers, three other stories—"Elsk meg bort fra min bristende barndom" ("Release Me Through Love From My Crumbling Childhood"), "Leken slutt" ("The End of the Game"), and "Vinterhav" ("Ocean in Winter")—conclude with union. In these stories Borgen reverses the familiar sex roles of his dreamer and seeker of reality. In "Elsk meg bort fra min bristende barndom" the woman is unwilling to cut the cord to the past. Her problem is similar to that of the protagonist in "Stjernen." Once adult reality fails her, she resorts to the world of imagination. In her mind, however, the concrete reality of love succeeds in suppressing the dream of returning to childhood. It rescues her from a fantasy world and resolves her crisis of identity. In "Leken slutt" Borgen's main character is a girl who has been obsessed since childhood with a desire to find the source of a river that flows through the village where she lives. The villagers know her fascination so well that they have started to call her by the same name as the river—"Synna." One day, virtually guided by instinct, she follows the river to the mountains and discovers that her path does not lead to a single source. Instead she finds many rivulets. She must continue to make her way through a landscape of slippery rocks before arriving at her destination, a tiny source surrounded by high, sharp cliffs. Exhausted, she kneels over the source and sees the reflection of her face in the water. For a time she remains fixed in this position. As darkness envelops her she is seized by an intense feeling of loneliness and imminent death. She is drawn to the water. Just as she is about to slide in, however, a human voice belonging to her lover restores her to reality. The spell of the stream is broken. She permits herself to be pulled toward safety and rests in the embrace of her lover's rescue.

It is probable that "Synna's" exploration of the river symbolizes her quest for the source of the self, while the cliffs represent the dangers one must pass through in order to reach the projected aim. "Synna" discovers that the unified, individualized self does not exist. Self-realization proves to be the equivalent of dissolution, death, and loss in the absolute. As night closes in on the girl kneeling over the water, the contours of her reflected face gradually disappear. She finds darkness, solitude, and imminent death. Having reached this point all choices seem closed to her except the final plunge into the water. But the voice of love pulls her from her trance and back to human reality.

The setting of "Vinterhav" is almost surrealistic. A young man is wandering through a dangerous, deserted landscape. It is an instinctive awareness of another human being in need that has drawn him from the safety of his village. A snowstorm rages. It no longer is clear where land ends and the sea begins. The man perceives another human shape and starts moving toward it. He reaches the second person, a woman with whom he engages in a fierce struggle. She tries to tear herself loose in order to reach the ocean: "Their breaths stand like woolen swords against each other, swords that blend with each other and melt into each other, a dagger from mouth to mouth."[14] The struggle becomes a literal one of life against death—the man representing summer and sunshine, the girl trying to pull herself toward the icy water: "He runs after her, and the fog starts lifting now that they have a little land around them. He keeps crying out: 'Look now! Don't you see the summer?' "[15] His evocation of the vision of summer is an attempt to show the girl that the benevolent side of human reality ultimately is more desirable than the wintry whiteness of dissolution. The man's vision prevails. The girl ceases her flight, and together the two return to the safety of the village.

Love therefore is a highly positive force in Borgen's short stories. "Fuglen og fristeren," where both lovers accept the dream and are destroyed by it, is exceptional. More commonly, love serves as the most important obstacle to immersion in psychological isolation, yearning for an absolute, and receptiveness to death. This does not mean that Borgen denies the value of the quest. However, he does appear to regret that the quest is death-oriented and therefore irreconcilable with lasting human happiness. While several of the love stories end with the union of the couple, rarely does Borgen indicate that the union will be permanent. In fact, only two stories describe a relatively happy couple living together for an extended period of time. "Stjernesang" ("Star Song") and "Livet går ikke videre" ("Life Does Not Continue") come most closely to such an ideal. In "Livet går ikke videre" a married pair live in a small town. Every evening the husband goes out to take a walk toward a tower located at some distance from the couple's house. The wife remains home, turns on a lamp, and attempts to pass the time reading. For the husband the light shining in the window at home represents a beacon that helps him find the road back from the tower. His wife's love, however, fails to cure him of his restless longing to escape reality. The tower and lamp illustrate the conflicting impulses that tempt one toward either isolation or love. The conflict between the two is never resolved in permanent fashion. In "Stjernesang" the husband feels an obsessive pull toward bridges, piers, train stations, and airports. The obsession is related to a memory of a childhood experience which had marked him deeply:

Once he had seen a dog drown. Three boys in a small sailboat were crossing against the wind. Then they saw a black setter, swimming away from land and struggling against the current. It was obvious that something had tempted it into the water and it proceeded to lose its feeling for land as dogs often do. They tried to cross towards it, slow down and drift with the wind as the dog turned while swimming. But each time they nearly reached it, in its desperate folly it would swim *away from* them instead of *towards* them. Twice it turned its wet head towards them, raised as high as possible to avoid the splashing of the waves. He never forgot that glance, so full of catastrophe and fear, yes, but also of longing for the destruction it was desperately trying to avoid, while its forelegs were whipping the sea.[16]

The dog's simultaneous fear of and longing for absorption represents the conflicting emotions Borgen's heroes feel toward death. Once the individual has experienced the temptation of the absolute, he no longer is free to return to a completely normal existence, even if he sincerely wishes it: "During a fatal moment it [the dog] had experienced the restless uncertainty of the human mind and had chosen a destruction which, once the chain linking it to life had loosened, it was not free to turn away from."[17] It is the same attraction-repulsion regarding the unknown that obsesses the husband in "Stjernesang." Unlike the dog, however, he does not sink. Whenever he is overwhelmed by longing, the thought of his wife strengthens his will to tear himself out of his trance and walk back to the house: "The stars in the sky did not concern him; nor did the train, nor the ships on the ocean."[18] The man is able to avoid the danger because he sees it clearly. The wife, on her side, realizes that her husband's restlessness is universal. Not even the couple's young child is spared. In this story, therefore, love helps the man and woman accept their human condition in a realistic way and live fulfilling, serene lives, aware of their dual nature.

Finally, in "Legende" ("Legend") Borgen suggests a poetic interpretation of the conflict. A man and woman stand on opposite cliffs facing one another. The landscape is surrealistic. Through signs and gestures each individual tries to communicate with the other. The man decides to head for the woman but loses sight of her, for she also has begun to move. Each character dreams of joining his partner in a beautiful bygone land, "a green plain traversed by the gleaming, blue river."[19] Finally, after very strenuous efforts both the man and the woman reach a plain and river, though at different times and not in the presence of the other. As each bends over the water to drink, he discovers a reflection of his own face ravaged by time. After another sip, a second face appears in the water. It is the image of the beloved, radiant and young. The vision fills the beholder with happiness and peace.

The journeys of the lovers symbolize their advance through time. Each travels alone and returns to the place of childhood, left many years earlier. As in the previous stories, the water represents the absolute into which the individual will be absorbed. Preceding death, however, is a moment of contemplation, when the individual leans over the pool and discovers his physical deterioration. The face of the beloved is spared such a fate. In the lover's memory it has remained young and beautiful.

The journeys of the man and the woman, undertaken in solitary fashion, illustrate the basic incompatibility between love and longing. Since the face of the beloved is saved from the decaying work of time, however, a compromise of sorts is attained; and separation manages to serve love.

In his short stories Borgen does not give a single answer to the dilemma served up by the conflict between love and longing. In spite of the life-affirming endings of "Hun ville det," "Leken slutt," and "Vinterhav," the total impression left by the stories may well be that the individual's most profound impulse is the quest for the source of the self. The protagonist in "Livet går ikke videre" was happy to be guided back home by his wife's lamp, but the next evening would find him again wandering off toward the tower. The couple in "Stjernesang," it is true, seem to have found a solution, but this story is quite unique. While love may provide invaluable flashes of happiness, it rarely offers a permanent solution for the individual who has experienced his crisis of consciousness.[20]

The conflict, moreover, must be seen within a broader framework of duality between dream and reality. The longing for the source of the self is a dream that humanity has always cherished. Love, on the other hand, is firmly rooted in the world of reality. In the novels from *Lillelord* through *Min arm, min tarm* the dream-reality conflict is of primary importance. The protagonist's attitude toward the problem and the manner in which he chooses to resolve it may serve as a key to the evolution of Borgen's thought during the two decades when he wrote his major novels.

CHAPTER 5

Flight from Community

THE publication of *Lillelord* (1955), *De mørke kilder* (1956) and *Vi har ham nå* (1957) marked Borgen's breakthrough as a major novelist. The trilogy relates the story of Wilfred Sagen, a talented musician, writer, and painter, the only son of a wealthy Oslo widow. Wilfred's mother smothers him with affection and deprives him of neither material nor cultural goods. Deeply experiencing the hypocrisy upon which conventional society is built, however, Wilfred becomes alienated from his family and class, and ultimately "drops out." A profound identity crisis seizes him and he alternately seeks and fears involvement with those who express a desire to help him resolve it. Physically and mentally, Wilfred becomes an outlaw engaged in a despairing search for the path that will restore him to his lost Eden, a homeland of innocence from which he believes himself to have been expelled.

The Danish novelist and critic H. C. Branner has underscored the thematic complexity of the *Lillelord* trilogy and has succinctly defined the multiple levels of meaning in the work:

On the surface it is an exciting novel of action, for Johan Borgen never forgets what is elementary. He knows that suspense is necessary to hold on to the reader. On the next level it is a description of the times—and an analysis of the times—stretching from the years prior to the First World War until the conclusion of the last one. Next it is a psychological description of high caliber. But at the core it has to do with a search for identity, borne out with an artistic consistency that shatters all of our conceptions of psychology.[1]

The thematic complexity of the trilogy clearly influences its form. A linear, realistic narrative, appropriate to the traditional social novel, vies for attention with a personal, symbolic narra-

64

tive that emphasizes the hero's metaphysical quest in a world without meaning. The critic is tempted to take exception to the admixture of styles and forms. Borgen's rejoinder might well be taken from his defense of Nordahl Grieg's equally complex play, *Vår ære og vår makt.* The form of Grieg's work, Borgen wrote, "simply mirrored the richness of the material. The images were linked together by a film technique that was highly effective."[2]

I *The Historical and Social Setting*

The life of Wilfred Sagen coincides almost exactly with the first forty-five years of the twentieth century. We follow him from the age of three and a half through his apparent suicide on the day of the Nazi capitulation in 1945. Borgen takes advantage of the setting to describe the fortunes of the comfortable Oslo bourgeoisie during three distinct periods—from around 1910–14, from 1914 to 1918, and during the years of the German ocupation, 1940–45.[3] During the time between the wars, of course, Norwegian politics and society underwent a profound transformation. The governing power of the bourgeois elite collapsed and was succeeded by the welfare state nurtured by the Labor Party. Borgen does not focus upon the vicissitudes of the repudiated leadership in the interwar years, however. He is primarily interested in the crisis that struck the governing classes when the period opened and in noting the response of the same individuals and certain *parvenus* to the new crisis that struck the land a generation later.

The problem of Norway's quest for a national identity seems to intrigue Borgen. Prior to 1914 a conservative, bourgeois leadership sat atop a highly stratified society where each group knew its place. During the First World War, however, a social crisis of severe magnitude struck neutral Norway. *Parvenus* engaged in the black market with the combatants and formed paper shipping companies supposedly intended to transport articles desperately needed by the warring sides. Having reaped fortunes dishonestly, the new rich used its money to infiltrate the old leadership. Lines separating the classes dissolved, the prewar elite was threatened, the country itself began to drift. To Borgen the subsequent emergence of the welfare state did little to redefine in a clear way Norway's national goals. The people themselves either were resisting the changes in the country or were busy adapting to them. They never were given the opportunity to ask themselves who they were or what their country's place in the world was supposed to be. Only the sense of community produced by resistance to the Germans during World War II gave meaning to the life of the nation. But it was a meaning born of crisis. It could hardly be expected to endure.

The *Lillelord* trilogy opens with pre-1914 society basking in the image of stability. At the summit are the great shipping, banking, fishing, and professional families, entrenched in their privileges and foreseeing no change in their leadership of the nation. Through the disruption in 1905 of the union with Sweden they had won full independence for Norway, and, incapable of comprehending a future remarkably different from the present, they now were consolidating their triumph. In effect, the leadership is in its adolescence. It vaguely senses gnawing social problems, but lacks the fortitude to place them in focus. But World War I changes everything. *De mørke kilder* deals with Norway's loss of innocence in the conflict. In his analysis of Nordahl Grieg's *Vår ære og vår makt*, Borgen sums up what occurred:

Operating under extremely dangerous conditions the neutral Norwegian merchant marine gained millions and millions of kroner—and brought home goods. This produced an era of profiteering the likes of which the country never before knew and hopefully will never again know. We saw young boys become millionaires in a week and jailbirds in a month. While Europe and America bled to death, our new rich rolled in champagne and caviar. The fancy hotels in the city became tinseled taverns and chic brothels, decent people on steady incomes lost their wits, committed forgery, founded fraudulent stock companies, embezzled funds, poured out thousand-kroner bills like sand, and lit their cigars with fifty-kroner notes. It is the most unworthy chapter in modern Norwegian history and had a demoralizing effect upon an entire generation.[4]

The period, when fortunes were quickly made or lost, fascinates Borgen. The word of the time was flexibility. Those of the old society who survived were the ones with sufficient moral adaptability to participate in the speculative game—individuals like Wilfred's uncle Martin, for whom wise investments give meaning to life. Barely out of their teens, Wilfred's schoolmates grow rich on the black market. One of them, Andreas, his pockets stuffed, treks off to Sweden and returns with a new family name and a claim to an aristocratic crest. To the *nouveaux riches* the war was a noisy party, replete with champagne, fireworks, and lottery prizes. When the armistice is signed, Oslo sinks into resignation, "filled with hangovers that follow the merry feast."

The interwar years in Norway, with the old social-political leadership diluted by the entrance of the profiteers into the ranks of the respectable, do not have a large role to play in the *Lillelord* trilogy. The bourgeoisie is edged out of power, its old economic privileges are eroded, and—along with the country— it drifts. *Vi har ham nå* takes place during the Second World War. Norway is occupied, and all elements in society—members of the old elite, former profiteers turned honest and respectable, Socialists, and the working classes—join together in a spirit of resistance. The country locates a sense of purpose, the society achieves a sense of integration.

But the *Lillelord* trilogy is not exclusively, or even essentially, an epic on the fate of the Norwegian upper classes or the search for national identity in the twentieth century. It fundamentally is the story of Wilfred Sagen, whose response to family, friends, society, and historical circumstance differs from everyone else's in the trilogy. Borgen shows how those closest to Wilfred adjust in their way to the crises of their times, but never the protagonist. Uncle Martin, in his striped suit, tries to profit from all the crises in which his country finds itself. Aunt Kristine becomes a humanitarian, and sentimental Uncle René goes to Paris in the middle of World War I in order to be with his beloved city in her hour of destiny. Wilfred's mother, Susanna Sagen, betrays the complacency of a large segment of her class during the years prior to World War I by refusing to change altogether. She builds a psychological dike against the flood tide of time. Borgen frequently portrays her standing by the closed window of her villa, looking out at the unchanging scenery. Her clothes are perfectly proper, though slightly out of fashion. Her face and figure retain their youthful freshness. Even during the war Susanna remains unmarked: "... It was as though the war and the stupidity of the world had passed by Mrs. Susanna Sagen without leaving a trace. During these years of distress out there in the wide world perhaps she had become a bit plumper, all her pretty curves even a bit more pleasantly rounded, but still she was without wrinkles and well-groomed to the point of defiance. And this, during a time when people took pride in suffering they did not themselves suffer, as though they felt themselves obliged to participate in suffering for the sake of decency."[5]

Susanna Sagen's pathetic resistance to change is exposed most clearly in her relationship to Wilfred, whose childhood she insists upon prolonging. She has him keep his long, ash-blond locks well into adolescence, and she makes him go through the seasonal ritual of hosting a children's ball even after he has outgrown that kind of pleasure. Wilfred accedes to his mother's wishes not out of a sense of submissiveness to her personality, but out of a habitual wish to please. As a child he performs the roles Susanna outlines for him. But during adolescence he gradually becomes alienated from her and her society. Attracted to the *parvenus* during the war, he amuses himself with the thought that the foundations of the old society are crumbling. He becomes a youthful cynic, repudiates his class, and takes up an extended stay among drug peddlers and gamblers in the Copenhagen underworld. He rejoices in the openness of the corruption he feels privileged to observe, in stark contrast with the respectable façade masking the hypocrisy of his bourgeois countrymen. Years later, when he sees his old friends, the profiteers of World War I, become the patriots of World War II, salving their consciences by virtue of their solidarity with a just cause, Wilfred becomes more cynical still. He refuses to acknowledge the sincerity of their behavior and, in morbid fascination for nihilism, is attracted to the Nazis. This marks his ultimate rejection of conventional Norwegian bourgeois society. But he cannot give himself completely to the new cause. A longing for childhood innocence has him identify with Nazi victims, and he aids a group of Jewish refugees to escape to neutral Sweden. The third volume of the *Lillelord* trilogy closes upon a triumphant note for Norway and her people. The Germans surrender, and Oslo explodes with joy. Wilfred finds himself in the capital. The country has attained a climactic moment of solidarity, but Wilfred cannot participate. Divorced from all social ideals, he experiences a sense of total loneliness, total solitude. Suspecting that he is a collaborator, the Resistance is after him. In a furnished room, facing his former girl friend who pleads with him to flee, he draws a gun and commits suicide. The act marks his escape from the world.

II *Roles and Masks*

Such a summary sketch of the historical setting in the *Lillelord* trilogy, and the place of certain major characters within this setting, cannot hope to do justice to the ambitious scope of the work. Its essential theme concerns Wilfred Sagen's flight from the values and roles his class instilled in him, his guilt for once having accepted them, and his pathetic quest for inner peace.[6] All through his life Wilfred senses nets being cast out to catch him. The earliest nets were those of his family. For Borgen, middle-class society needs its ceremonies where each member is expected to conform to his specific role. The family reunion that opens the trilogy illustrates this well. As he awaits the arrival of his mother's guests, the fourteen-year-old Wilfred anticipates the rite of welcome that will take place. Topped by his long ash-blond locks and shod in his patent leather pumps, Wilfred will stand in the center of the drawing room playing the perfect little host. All the guests will then perform their parts. The effeminate Uncle René will admire his well-groomed mustache in the mirror and chatter a few words in French. To counteract René's possible influence upon Wilfred, Uncle Martin will launch into a reminder on the virtues of masculinity. Aunt Klara will play her game of exaggerated self-effacement.

Role-playing is symptomatic of the fundamental illness of society, namely, its lack of honesty. Early in life the bright child learns that the adult world is less interested in him as a human being than as a performer. It seeks the delicately made artificial nightingale rather than the genuine bird.[7] Susanna Sagen desires Wilfred to possess impeccable manners. Martin would like him to become a businessman in the uncle's own image. René wishes for Wilfred to become a Norwegian Mozart so as to grace his musical salon. The child's natural inclination is to please, and consequently he learns his parts to perfection. He discovers easily enough that skillful role-playing is the key to mastery of his environment. During oral examinations at school, to which the children's parents are invited, Wilfred dazzles his audience with a flawless performance. But worse perhaps than even the social pressures for the child to excel are the destructive forces unleashed within his psyche. Wilfred is terrorized by the thought of losing in competition. He must supplement his natural talent with tricks and ploys until he becomes such an expert player that he can manipulate his role at will. Indeed, this is the first sign of remorse for having played it at all. During a student recital Wilfred selects a sexually risqué folk ballad in order to measure the shock effect upon his audience. He even turns to petty crimes and then escapes suspicion through magnificent performances. He enjoys deceiving others by assuming various parts that will gain him the advantage he seeks. Ultimately, however, Wilfred's guilt becomes overwhelming. He envisions himself as wearing a perpetual mask that bears the inscription "I am false." He begins to resent the role as Mozart and turns down René's invitations to play. He considers himself to have been transformed into a lifeless puppet, or an empty shell containing interchangeable parts that form a variety of "personalities." A realization of his enslavement to the cult of success adds to Wilfred's alienated state. He longs for authenticity. An outsider to himself, his society, and his surroundings, the boy becomes schizoid. He undergoes a crisis of identity.

The *Lillelord* trilogy relates Wilfred's tormented search for an authentic self. As a child he already felt the need to break out of the net into which his social environment had placed him: "An entire world of possibilities was waiting; filled with sin, with sins."[8] As a young man he flees his family for the Copenhagen underworld. The conflicting forces inside Wilfred surface violently. He becomes angel and devil, humanitarian

and Nazi, executioner and victim. The divisions he feels within
the self give rise to a Hamlet-like indecisiveness. Unable to will
the adoption or elimination of elements in his personality,
Wilfred finds that he can do nothing except keep options open.
Confused and guilt-ridden, he nevertheless maintains his quest.

III   *From Childhood to the Fall*

As we have previously noted, Borgen customarily links the
quest for identity with nostalgia for childhood. Prior to sub-
mission to the roles expected of him, the child can experience
emotions without sham. His fall from innocence is inevitable,
but the degree of alienation varies from individual to individual.
Those who get caught in society's web—that is, the overwhelming majority of humanity—feel it minimally, because they are
living wholly unconscious lives. And those who remain uncomplicated enough to keep a few links to childhood feel it
minimally also, for they manage to stay in touch with parts
of their authentic selves. In Borgen's work they may include
an Uncle René or several female characters. On the other hand,
most of Borgen's male protagonists experience their "fall" keenly.
They suffer guilt from it and in a fumbling way seek means of
extricating themselves from their torment through self-mortifi-
cation or confession. Borgen's novels customarily follow the
cyclical movement of the hero's fall, his terrifying exile in the
shadow-world of society, his wrenching away from this existence,
and finally his labored journey back in time toward what the
author calls "the place." The peregrinations of Borgen's heroes
resemble vaguely the wanderings of the protagonists in Beckett's
novels or the journey of the Unknown in Strindberg's *Road to
Damascus I*. Though Borgen's basic theme seems to be a pilgrim's
progress, his protagonists neither seek nor find salvation in a
Christian sense. Their universe is devoid of God.

In Borgen's work the image of the falling child frequently
reappears. Wilfred's earliest recollection concerns an episode
that occurred when he was three and a half years old. At a
family picnic his father playfully threw him into the air. Wilfred
recalls that for a split second he sensed he was falling to his
death. Though he landed safely in his father's arms, in reliving

the scene in his mind Wilfred no longer is certain whether his father actually did catch him. The scene is an extremely important one and forms a kind of *leitmotif* in the trilogy. Wilfred's belief that he may have fallen is caused by the fact that two years after the picnic incident the elder Sagen committed suicide. As the boy grew up, he considered his father's death to be an act of betrayal. Because of this he often has the occasion to contrast the filial experiences of others with his own. For example, one day he observes a team of acrobats rehearsing its act in Copenhagen's Tivoli amusement park. A child member of the troupe is supposed to leap from a perch into the arms of his father who is swinging by his feet from a pair of rings below. But the boy frequently misses his goal and falls into the protective net. The father and other family members watching reprove the boy, and Wilfred is greatly upset by their attitude. But the little acrobat continues practicing until he ultimately masters the act. Again and again he reaches his father's arms. The rehearsal thus concludes successfully; and the acrobats leave the stage: "Father and son followed the others, the father had his hand on the boy's head."[9] Parental confidence has taught the boy to respect his own abilities. On the other hand, instead of channeling him into a place in society that could withstand doubts and questions, Wilfred's father abandoned the boy to the alternating protectiveness and permissiveness of Susanna. Lacking the support of a firm authority, Wilfred found his bitterness grow and sense of social alienation increase. Wilfred's plight resembles the situation Sartre, who lost his father at a very early age, describes in *Les Mots*.[10] Resenting the masks and roles which society attempted to impose upon him, the child merely drifted along without any sense of identity. Interestingly enough, the elder Sagen had also rejected Susanna and her circle. He had fled to the forest cabin of his mistress, Mrs. Frisaksen—and to the social isolation it represented.

In another sense Borgen suggests that the pattern of Wilfred's plight may be inherited from his father. The possibility exists that, when he threw the child into the air, the elder Sagen harbored a latent desire to have Wilfred drop to the ground rather than grow up in a society the father was at the verge of rejecting. The infanticide theme reappears in the trilogy. By implication Wilfred shares the guilt of one of his early mistresses who destroys the foetus of their unborn child. Later, during a police raid upon a Copenhagen narcotics and gambling den, Wilfred escapes with the baby of one of his prostitute acquaintances. For several months he cares for the infant. One day, however, he is seized by a passion to kill it: "Like a thief he plunged into the warm padding of the baby carriage and seized the child who was lying there. Wildly triumphant, he raised it above his head and made ready to fling it against the rock."[11] But Wilfred cannot murder the infant. Instead, he hands it over to a childless couple with whom he is living, and disappears. The parallel with his father of possible murderous intent, followed by abandonment, is striking.

Conflicting urges to destroy and save children are central to Wilfred's psychological dilemma. He is painfully aware of having killed the child he used to be. A symbolic child murderer, in his quest for authenticity he contemplates becoming one in fact. Then at least his mask will be off and his guilt exposed for all to see. It is far easier, however, for Wilfred to theorize such a radical solution than to bring it about. The will to seek redemption by saving lives more than balances the desire to curse the world by taking them. On an occasion in Paris he offers a merry-go-round ride to a child. She accidentally slips and falls into the ride's mechanism. Instinctively Wilfred reaches into the grinding machinery and pulls her out unhurt. In the process, however, he loses his own right hand. Years later, in the midst of the Second World War, the Germans select him to guard a group of Jews—childlike in their innocence and bewilderment—caught while trying to escape to Sweden. Rather than become party to their extermination, instinctively Wilfred directs them to safety.

But saving children does not save Wilfred. His self-contempt is all-consuming. He prefers the company of criminals to that of the respectable bourgeoisie. He tries to distort his fair, handsome face with grimaces that become part of him. He deeply senses his unauthenticity, and the clawlike mechanism that has replaced his right hand means more to him than his own left one. He considers his humanity to be denied. This is effectively symbolized in another episode in Paris, when he enters an exercise parlor and observes individuals engaged in a puppetlike walk. He joins them, and nearly in a trance, performs the movement to perfection. Again in Paris, he finds himself in a nightclub where he observes a couple dancing the Charleston. His own body begins to shake and jerk like a mechanical doll out of control. In his uncontrollable movements he finds a strange, liberating sensation.

IV   *The Quest for Identity*

Considering himself to be betrayed by his father, Wilfred Sagen is incapable of steering a course for his own personality. Though he discovers early in childhood that he really is not "Lillelord," the artificial nightingale whose function would be to please others through his own brilliance, this side of Wilfred fails to disappear completely. All through his life, whenever he encounters an individual from his youth, almost instinctively Wilfred reverts to an attitude of exaggerated politesse. The realization of this only intensifies his self-contempt, and he confronts his guilt through worship of what is ugly and deformed. When such behavior fails to satisfy him he desperately tries to find a means of acquiring a spirit of purity and innocence. He drifts from attitude to attitude without finding a consistent pattern of behavior; and he drifts from métier to métier without developing his potential in a single one. Between the wars he lives for some time in Paris as a painter. But his canvases have a puzzling, incomplete quality that baffles the beholder. Thoroughly unable to discover on his own who he is, Wilfred is constantly on the lookout for a surrogate father. He successively chooses Uncle René, the Danish artist Børge Hviid, his friend Robert, and the writer Knut Hamsun. None, however, helps him. Wilfred most resembles a pitiful Hamlet, unable to choose among multiple inclinations, vaguely sensing a message that the parental ghost has for him but which he cannot interpret.[12] Wilfred experiences life as a prolonged set of falls. Others cast out nets to catch him as he plunges. When they are successful, Wilfred struggles to escape, falls, and is caught anew. He cannot find liberty and fears finding it. Ultimately he resigns himself to entrapment.

We already have noticed the nets that various social groups

place beneath him: first the family's, then the friends', subsequently the criminals', and finally the Nazis'. Individuals drop nets as well. At the end of *De mørke kilder* Wilfred makes a suicide attempt that never comes off. Robert, a friend from his youth, senses that Wilfred is in a depressed state and wishes to help him. Wilfred responds by fleeing. Robert was one of those who had gained a dubiously earned fortune during World War I. During the German occupation of 1940–45, however, he helps the Resistance. In the war he again wishes to assist Wilfred, in large measure because he knows that the Underground suspects his old friend of being a collaborator. Almost against his better judgment, Robert becomes a kind of savior. He cares for Wilfred's paintings and provides him with a place of refuge. Wilfred accepts Robert's assistance, but without gratitude. He refuses to commit himself to Robert's cause and values, even if it means saving his own life. His hiding place becomes yet another trap, his final one.

Wilfred's contemptuous behavior toward Robert is perhaps partly based on a feeling of superiority. It is also based on a fear that the friend might betray him, just as his father had done. For a long time he is fascinated by the thought of his half-brother Birger, the son of his father and Mrs. Frisaksen. He wishes Birger, whom he has never met, to be a real brother, someone who shares Wilfred's family name and wealth. Subsequently, his mood changes completely, he develops a hostility toward Birger, and ultimately betrays his half-brother to the Germans during the occupation. Birger dies in a concentration camp. Betrayal is Wilfred's instinctive response when he feels his solitude threatened.

More dangerous than Birger is Moritz, a German officer stationed in an obscure post in occupied Norway. Moritz is a typical character in the tradition of decadent Romanticism.[13] He has a background similar to Wilfred's, exhibits an artistic temperament, and is in exile in a foreign, hostile land. He comprehends the contradictions within his own personality and is completely cynical about them. Better than anyone else, he also understands Wilfred's conflicting desires to be entrapped and to flee. He nourishes the hope of forming with his Norwegian double a community of outcasts. Wilfred knows that Moritz is after him.

He sees the familiar net in the German's eyes. First attracted magnetically to Moritz, Wilfred subsequently rejects him with a violence born of fear. When he realizes that he has failed to entice his prey, Moritz tries a final, desperate ploy. He attempts to get Wilfred to kill him. This too fails, ultimately, and the German dies from a self-inflicted wound. Wilfred obtains his liberty, but Moritz's example offers him the suggestion that perhaps his own death will provide him with genuine freedom.

Wilfred has no regrets for being separated from Moritz. The relationship was constructed upon the German's need for a double with whom he could share his cynicism and nihilism. The entrapment he offered Wilfred promised to be one of the damned. After one of his encounters with Moritz, Wilfred, however, recalled a much more promising possibility that had come to him years earlier, and that he had stupidly rejected. That was the possibility of rescuing a wasted life through love: "He sat there looking at his wax-colored hand. He found himself back in a world where perhaps he should have stayed. . . . He had fled then too, towards the catastrophe inside himself, away from the possible, away from the real. He sat there and suddenly knew it. And it was too late. Good God. It was too late. . . ."[14] Because it intruded upon his quest for solitude, Wilfred had extricated himself from the net of love. The affair concerned Miriam, a young Jewish violinist whom he had known when both were studying at the conservatory in Oslo, and who several years later rescued him from the den of thieves, addicts, and prostitutes with whom he had fallen in during his Copenhagen experience. Subsequently the pair met again in Paris, lived together there, and passed a few idyllic autumn weeks in Brittany.

Miriam is present in all three volumes of the trilogy, but it is not until *Vi har ham nå* that Borgen describes her at length. She is allowed a point of view through which, twenty years later, she recalls her affair with Wilfred. As a character she provides some instructive similarities and contrasts with Wilfred. In the first place, she belongs to a people whose vague longings for a lost land comprise a cardinal point in their collective history. Nevertheless, Miriam's simplicity and inner peace are wholly the obverse of Wilfred's complexity and restlessness. She possesses a contented sense of solidarity with her family. Her talent and artistic achievement bring her a sincere feeling of fulfillment. During the war, when her life hangs in the balance, her resourcefulness and self-confidence permit her to prevail.

As very young music students, Wilfred and Miriam had been attracted to one another. At the conservatory in Oslo she played the violin and he the piano. Their paths then diverged. While Wilfred never developed his potential as a pianist, Miriam became a well-known violinist, giving performances in all the great cities of Europe. Like Robert, only in a more profound sense, Miriam is a savior-figure for Wilfred. In difficulty with his criminal acquaintances who believe he has betrayed them, Wilfred must flee the gang through the streets of Copenhagen. During the pursuit he spies a theater marquee announcing a concert by Miriam. Wilfred barges into the rear-door entrance of the concert hall while Miriam is on stage, finds her dressing room unlocked, and goes inside. Miriam arrives, cares for Wilfred, drives him to her apartment, and later helps him arrange his trip back to Oslo. But Wilfred experiences Miriam's goodness as a threat. Having collapsed into a chair filled with bouquets from her admirers, Wilfred had the sensation of dying and being buried beneath her flowers. In the back seat of her car he felt as if he were confined in a coffin.[15] Several years later, after the couple have met again in Paris and pass a fall vacation in Brittany, Miriam helps save Wilfred from drowning—from being carried off into the solitude of the sea. The episode bears resemblance to that of the drowning dog in "Stjernesang." Symbolically, Miriam's act is supposed to save Wilfred from all the destructive forces within himself. But Miriam finds it impossible to hold him when his will longs to escape. Following the time in Brittany the pair return to Paris. There Wilfred sees himself as a mechanical doll, his humanity denied, still unable to come to terms with his identity. He exposes his latest paintings to Miriam and she shrinks back in shock and revulsion. The canvases are enormous, profoundly disturbing mechanical-like abstractions that appear to deny Miriam's simple formula that life is love and love is sharing. Perhaps she fails to perceive Wilfred's art as a cry of agony and a plea for understanding. Borgen views the romance of the couple as a struggle between two private visions of existence. For the relationship to endure one of the partners must renounce his vision and allow himself to be engulfed by the other. Wilfred's quest for identity, illustrated in his art, causes Miriam to feel herself dissolving, losing command over her personality, and falling under the influence of laws that imprison her spirit. Wilfred's quest betrays not only the couple's love for one another, but also life as Miriam beholds it: "I stood there and was filled with hatred, but also with something more, a hopelessness that knew neither bounds nor exit. Spontaneously, a word formed within me: treason. . . ."[16] If she is to retain her own simplicity, Miriam understands that she will have to break with Wilfred. He threatens to overwhelm her. "My solitude—I clung to it as a point of departure. *His* solitude was—arrogant, an attack."[17] Yet Miriam's love is strong enough to withstand her initial revulsion. Perhaps she can prevail, she thinks. It is Wilfred who breaks off the relationship. "Live well," he writes to her. To her sorrow, Miriam recalls how the forces of destruction "kept pulling Wilfred away from her—"As if the forces out there had a firmer grasp upon him than I could maintain, however tightly I held on."[18]

Miriam's failure to keep Wilfred reveals the incompatibility between her love and his longing. On the other hand, Wilfred's entrapment by Mrs. Frisaksen, his father's one-time mistress, aids him in retracing the route he seeks back to the "place" of authenticity.[19] As an adolescent, Wilfred liked to withdraw to Mrs. Frisaksen's humble, isolated cabin in the woods, sensing perhaps that the old woman was an intermediary between himself and his lost father. Even before Wilfred forsook his family and friends, Mrs. Frisaksen had presented him with a glass egg that had belonged to the elder Sagen. Inside the egg was the representation of a path leading to a house through a snowy landscape. For the scene to remain clear the egg had to be held perfectly still. If the egg were moved or shaken, the scene would become obscured. Later in life Wilfred would find himself returning to the abandoned cabin of Mrs. Frisaksen and, holding the egg, contemplating the place. He learns that the house within the egg, like the cabin itself, represents "the place"—the objective of all Borgen heroes. Complete inaction renders it visible. Symbolically then, the egg suggests a return to utter passivity. If the foetal state is an impossible dream, at least restoration with mother earth is within comprehension.

Of all the characters in the trilogy Mrs. Frisaksen alone provides Wilfred with a sense of peace. The first important meeting between the two occurred when Wilfred was a teen-ager and had been swimming fully clothed in the sea. He alights upon an island, removes his things and places them down to dry. While resting, naked, he spots Mrs. Frisaksen's rowboat approaching his place of refuge. She is on her way to perform her job, the inspection of the beacons of the lighthouse on the island. Wilfred makes no attempt to cover his nakedness—as he would have done had anyone else appeared. Instead he exchanges a few words with the woman, and then she rows away. As Wilfred observes Mrs. Frisaksen move off toward the sunset, she appears transformed into "a little woman in a bowl of gold."[20] What impresses Wilfred is the fact that Mrs. Frisaksen is whole, self-contained, utterly independent of society and its forms: "She was one and indivisible, a safe but solitary outcast in a boat."[21] Whenever Wilfred will feel the nets of others descending upon him, he will start longing for Mrs. Frisaksen: "[She] *was the one who didn't give a damn about anything.* Who didn't give a damn, a damn, a damn about anything! Who had enough in her own microscopic existence."[22] In fact, Wilfred believes that Mrs. Frisaksen possesses the absolute peace that he is constantly looking for, and that he will discover only in death.

A macabre experience near the end of the first volume of the trilogy presages the resolution of Wilfred's problem. Fleeing from school and his family, he has an urge to visit the old woman. In a scene recalling the theme of the glass egg, he becomes lost in a blinding snow storm. Finally he reaches Mrs. Frisaksen's cabin. Exhausted, he crawls around it to find the door, enters at last, and discovers the woman dead in her bed. After looking unsuccessfully for someone who might assist him with her body, Wilfred returns to the cabin, removes his wet clothes, and wraps himself in Mrs. Frisaksen's fishing net. Later he will recall the net as something peaceful, "that neither entrapped nor threatened."[23] He climbs into bed, snuggles against the corpse, and falls into a deep sleep. In life Mrs. Frisaksen had been Wilfred's beacon. Her fishing net signified safety. The egg she gave him contained a lesson. Her final message for Wilfred is for him to seek out peace through the elimination of consciousness, in death. It is the elder Sagen's message as well. It takes Wilfred another thirty years to appreciate it—a generation of longing, self-torment, entrapments, and escapes—before he attains release.

In so doing Wilfred rejects his social class, Robert's friendship, and Miriam's love. He sees other people as threats to his solitude. His quest fails to return him to the innocence of childhood, and he finds peace only in death. All through his life, however, Wilfred toys with an option which might permit him to possess his solitude and yet continue to live. This is through self-expression in art. In *Innbilningen og kunsten,* Borgen discussed the relationship between the quest for identity and the vocation of the artist. Wilfred has extraordinary potential as a pianist, painter, and writer. But he is no more committed to his art than to either friendship or love. Initially, however, he tried. As very young men both Wilfred and Robert carried copies of Hamsun's *Pan* in their pockets. Unlike Robert, Wilfred never completely renounces the dream of *Pan,* but neither does he fully comprehend what Hamsun is telling him. At one point, toward the end of *De mørke kilder,* Wilfred thought he had an opportunity to learn the poet's message in direct fashion. He and the writer were staying at the same hotel in the country. While walking in the forest near the hotel, Wilfred saw Hamsun. He watched the writer stop, pull a piece of paper out of his pocket, and quickly write something on it with a pencil. Then Hamsun walked on. Hamsun repeated this sequence several times.[24]

At dinner time Wilfred sees Hamsun again in the hotel's dining room. Overwhelmed by emotion, he feels that he is closer to "the place" than ever before and desires to introduce himself. At a loss for words, however, he stumbles to his feet and quietly leaves the room. He senses that Hamsun is thankful for being left alone. The next morning he learns that the writer has checked out of the hotel. Wilfred returns to the forest and in vain tries to retrieve the mood that he had felt the day before: "It was as if the wing of a powerful bird had brushed him, a father."[25] But the experience eludes him. Wilfred never again has an opportunity to communicate with the writer. "But if he had ventured to ask about his [Hamsun's] innermost sensation of everything, then perhaps he would have discovered the profoundly sad glance one knew from photographs, the glance which said that the sum of all his enormous experiences may nevertheless resemble a nothingness with no end and no beginning...."[26] Of course, the artist's quest had not necessarily brought him closer to solving the problem of existence, and the sum of his many experiences was nothing. Yet, on that day in the forest Hamsun was smiling and humming to himself as he jotted down words on his note pad. His art seems to have filled the void of his life and given it a touch of sense. Wilfred, however, fails to reach this point. As he betrays all else, he betrays his artistic calling. Shortly before his suicide, again walking through a forest, Wilfred by chance enters the house of a family whose members had understood his paintings and even consider Wilfred Sagen to be a spiritual guide of sorts. As the father and daughter receive him and offer him their hospitality, Wilfred feels a momentary sense of warmth and solidarity. But he discovers the impossibility of sharing the family's peaceful resignation built upon an awareness of life's emptiness. "They could not show him any road."[27] He is overwhelmed with scorn for his hosts, steals a crystal container filled with whiskey, and flees. He mirthfully remarks to himself how good it feels to disappoint these well-meaning people, and disappears into the woods.

V *Conclusion*

The second and third volumes of the *Lillelord* trilogy bring Wilfred closer and closer to the type of peace Mrs. Frisaksen mapped out for him near the conclusion of volume one. But he must make his wearisome journey confronting society, friendship, love, guilt, art, and the will to live itself. Pulled between the egg and the world, Wilfred becomes a mental and physical wreck. In the latter part of *Vi har ham nå* he is a specter of his former self: "All parts protruded—mouth, nose, forehead—protruded from the cavities of the cheeks; they looked as though they had their base far inside the cavity of the mouth itself. The gray-blond hair hung dead around the meager temples, and the hand he offered was like a claw to touch."[28] Just prior to his suicide Wilfred wanders through a physical Purgatory—a cold, dark forest with hills and threatening crevices, a country unfit for humans, "the land that God had failed to reach." This represents the climactic moment of Wilfred's voyage through life. The No-man's Land in which he wanders is Nobiskro, a Norwegian derivation of a German colloquialism for Purgatory: "But to the elect there came the sneaking suspicion that Nobiskro represents their present life—an intermediary state, filled with unclear recollections and painful forebodings, recollections about the past, forebodings about the future."[29] While Nobiskro, with its endless boredom, is an image of contemporary life, only the individual who has undergone a crisis of consciousness suffers from it. In Nobiskro the individual prepares himself for death. Wilfred wanders off to the site of Mrs. Frisaksen's cabin. He realizes that he is approaching the journey's end and hopes for a new message—perhaps one that may strengthen him and give him courage to meet the death that he still fears. But the cabin has fallen into ruin. Nothing remains.

Wilfred abandons his upright stance. He crawls about. He finds a cave where he had earlier sought refuge and enters like a wild animal. A spider weaves a net at the cave's mouth. Wilfred hopes to die peacefully. But his body betrays his wishes, and hunger drives him from his chosen tomb. With regrets he breaks the spider's net and withdraws from the cave. Yet he decides that he will flee no more. He returns to Oslo where he intends to give himself up as a collaborator to the Resistance. His sole desire is to "lie down, only to lie down." His return to the city coincides with the German surrender. Oslo is brimming over with joy. Having decided to give up his flight, Wilfred too is celebrating a victory of sorts. He goes to the room where Robert has let him live and discovers Miriam there. She has rushed back from exile in Sweden and again offers to save Wilfred. She pleads with him to get out of Oslo, for the Underground is combing the city for suspected collaborators. In Wilfred's eyes Miriam is transformed into a shining light, the beacon perhaps that he should have followed many years earlier. Now it is too late: "A numbness overwhelmed him, something almost without feeling, as when one has been swimming too long. That was it! He had been swimming too long. He had been swimming and swimming. It was time to sink."[30] As the couple hear the steps of Wilfred's pursuers in the stairwell, he rejects Miriam's final plea to run. He sticks both hands in his pockets; one grabs the glass egg, the other Moritz's revolver. Without knowing whether the weapon is loaded or not, he pulls the trigger and a shot goes off. The voice of the pursuer rings out: "We have got him now!" On this note of irony the novel ends.

The conclusion of the trilogy is ambiguous. Borgen fails to make clear whether Wilfred consciously commits suicide or simply drifts into death. In any event, death signifies acceptance of Mrs. Frisaksen's message. It represents the only possible termination of Wilfred's quest, since he had gradually eliminated all other options. The words of the Resistance worker are hollow. This time the pursuers' net holds only a corpse. Wilfred's self is beyond human reach. It is absorbed in the universe from which it originally had sprung.

CHAPTER 6

Art as Compromise

LIKE Wilfred Sagen, Matias Roos—the protagonist of "*Jeg*"—
is a restless wanderer in search of a lost homeland. In
spiritual exile, he longs to recross the frontier separating him
from his place of origin. But the frontier is vague and always
seems to slip away from his grasp. In his quest Matias remains
frustrated. He has experienced a falling-away from authenticity,
struggles against a sensation of profound guilt, and eventually
obtains a kind of peace in resignation. Matias, however, never
reaches the goal for which he was searching.

Unlike the trilogy, "*Jeg*" is wholly experimental in form. In
writing it, Borgen appears to have been inspired by Kafka.
Indeed, "*Jeg*" contains many echoes of *The Trial*.[1] While he
needed three volumes to relate the story of Wilfred Sagen,
Borgen has condensed the narration of Matias's quest to 241
pages. The setting is Europe, rebuilt after World War II. An
alliance between technology and capitalism has produced material prosperity but, in Borgen's view, at the cost of controlling
the lives and dictating the happiness of countless millions. In
Scandinavia, by virtue of its benevolent caress, the welfare
state has overwhelmed the individaul as well, and Bureaucracy
is incapable of responding to basic human needs. In "*Jeg*" the
social commentary never detracts from the novel's central theme.
In fact, it throws additional light on Matias's alienation, renders
his guilt more comprehensible, and underscores the necessity of
the quest for identity.

The structure of "*Jeg*" resembles that of a Freudian dream.
The opening pages illustrate the split in Matias's personality. Its
two sides are described as "I" and "he." "I"—the side of the
personality that is left behind—describes the vicissitudes of
"he"—the active agent. Borgen's technique seems to illustrate
Freud's theory of personality dissociation in the course of a

dream. The dreamer tries to resolve his psychological conflict by witnessing from the outside the estranged part of himself. Visualizing his problem in this way, the dreamer contributes to the resolution of the problem upon which the dream is based.[2] In *"Jeg"* the split in the protagonist's personality is evident from the very first paragraph. The passive side of the self, "I," observes the departure of the active side. During the first half of the novel the distance between the two sides increases. During the second half the distance tends to close. And in the final paragraph the two parts merge: "I emerge from my place at the edge of the forest. Before we meet we are one. He becomes me."[3]

The time passing between the first and final pages of *"Jeg"* covers a summer and four subsequent years. About the four years, during which Matias serves a prison sentence, Borgen says virtually nothing. The crucial time period of the novel has to do with several selected days of a summer preceding Matias's imprisonment and the two days following his release four years later. Much of the book consists of conversations Matias holds before his imprisonment with a young social worker named Sonja or her landlady Mrs. Skarseth. The most important of these conversations takes place in a cafeteria, where the fifty-six-year-old Matias relates the story of his life to Sonja. Rather than deliver a straight narrative, he relates episodic fragments. The earliest of the episodes occurred when he was fourteen, and by the time he completes his tale he has covered his life in a mosaic dealing with the years from adolescence to late middle age.

In *"Jeg"* a fragmentation of space accompanies the fragmentation of time. The places where Matias finds himself during the various parts of the novel are few and carefully selected: his home in the forest, a hotel, a lecture hall, a rooming house, a park outside the city, a cafeteria. Matias frequently is either cycling or walking along a road that connects two of these locations. In the story he relates to Sonja, Matias regards space in an equally economical way. A very important setting for his tale is an inn at a frontier post. The inn carries the familiar Borgen name, Nobiskro. Other places about which Matias speaks are his childhood home, particularly its attic, where his family had stored away an old English chair; a prison; a summer hotel. In the novel the rural settings (the house in the forest, the child-

hood home, a park Matias visits with Sonja) are contrasted with
the urban settings (the hotel, the prison, a lecture hall). Happiness, or at least resigned peace, is associated with the country
places; exile with the city ones.

I *The Plot*

Despite a fragmented narrative the plot of *"Jeg"* is relatively
simple to follow. On a spring day Matias Roos leaves his house
in the forest, picks up a motorcycle at a nearby farm, and starts
off on a journey to town. On the road Matias thinks he has hit
a small child who ran in front of his cycle. He makes note of the
child's grandmother, who had been sitting outside knitting when
the accident occurred. She leaps from her chair and screams.
The empty chair and the knitting, a child's sweater with an
unfinished sleeve, will form a leitmotif in the novel. Without
stopping at the scene of the accident, Matias continues his journey to town. Upon arriving he goes directly to the police and
declares himself guilty of manslaughter. But an investigation
of the accident refutes Matias's confession. First the officers
declare that it was the child's fault, later they maintain that no
accident ever occurred. Frustrated at having been turned away
by the police, Matias settles into a hotel room and occupies his
evenings with alcohol and women. One morning, filled with self-
contempt, he leaves the hotel. The sunshine outside becomes
intolerable, and he enters a lecture hall where an individual is
making a spirited defense of a certain Teodor, accused of having
murdered his father-in-law. The speech angers Matias, and he
leaves the hall muttering that the guilty merit punishment. At
this juncture Matias encounters Sonja, a young psychologist
employed as a social worker. The two become friends, and in
the course of the summer their friendship matures into love.
In an important episode Matias visits the rooming house where
Sonja lives and holds a lengthy conversation with her landlady,
Mrs. Skarseth. The latter tells him about her daughter, Johanna,
the unwed mother of a little girl. Johanna holds a teaching job
in the north of Norway. It is clear that while Mrs. Skarseth had
always urged Johanna to become a liberated woman, she never
really loved her daughter. She thrusts all her affection upon

Sonja, whom she considers her spiritual child. At the conclusion
of Part I of the novel, Sonja and Matias sit in a cafeteria, where
the girl urges her friend to tell her the story of his life. Reluc-
tantly, Matias does so; but he warns Sonja that he no longer
is the Matias he used to be, and that memory tends to betray
reality, turning it into fiction.

The second part of "*Jeg*"—129 of the novel's 241 pages—is
devoted entirely to Matias's story-confession. Part of his story
concerns a journey he believes he took to a mysterious border
crossing. Matias uses the third person, as though to underscore
the distance he feels between his present and his former self.
Matias tells how the border guards refused to accept his identification papers, turned him away, and told him to take a room at
an inn on the frontier. The inn was called Nobiskro.[4] Within it
Matias discovered people who resembled individuals he had
once known. From Matias's story Sonja also learns that he had
been a gifted chemist and had sold his skills to a group of
politicians engaged in treasonous activities. Subsequently Matias's
involvement cost him several years in prison. Upon his release
his troubles were not over. He became involved in an act of
terrorism and turned fugitive. He thinks of himself as an outlaw,
a restless voyager, a perpetual denizen of Nobiskro—No-man's
Land—"where people wander between life and death in a kind
of prolonged caricature of existence."[5] There is no reason to
doubt that the mental state Matias describes in his story is
different from the one he actually feels as he relates it. His
behavior is characterized by restlessness and a strong sensation
of guilt. Though society apparently has lost interest in Matias's
crimes, he very clearly has not. He is seeking a way to redeem
himself for having committed them.

Part III is symmetrical with Part I. It describes Matias's
attempt to escape from the Nobiskro of his soul. On finishing
the story he accompanies Sonja to Mrs. Skarseth's rooming
house. He learns that Johanna has returned home. After supper
Sonja retires to her room, and a few minutes later Matias follows
her. He finds her dead on her bed, smothered by a pillow.
Jealous of her mother's affection for Sonja, Johanna murdered
the girl. Matias, however, assumes Johanna's guilt, stands trial,
and is sentenced to prison for six years. He serves four of them

and wins parole. The story resumes on the day of his release. Instinctively, Matias heads directly for Mrs. Skarseth's rooming house. Upon entering, he learns that she has moved to a place on the city's outskirts. He finds it, and, unobserved, witnesses a tender scene between Mrs. Skarseth and her young granddaughter. Matias goes no further. He leaves and returns to his house in the forest.

"*Jeg*" follows a perfectly circular plot outline and may be diagramed in the following manner:

The house in the forest.

"I" and "he" split apart.   "I" and "he" reunite.

The farm. Matias picks up his   The farm.
motorcycle.

The accident. The empty chair.   The reconciliation of child and
The discarded knitting. Matias   grandmother. The knitting is
declared innocent.   gone.

Meeting with Sonja.   Matias declared guilty.
                                  Sonja's murder.
The conversation with Mrs.
Skarseth. She mentions Jo-   The conversation with Mrs.
hanna.   Skarseth. Johanna's return.

In the cafeteria. Sonja asks   In the cafeteria. Sonja medi-
Matias to relate his story.   tates upon Matias's story.

Matias's story,
a novel within the novel.

The relation by Matias of his life story is the turning point in the novel. Having finished his long tale, Matias may begin undertaking his redemptive journey home. Moreover, all the major episodes illuminate the themes of crime and punishment, guilt and atonement.

II   *The Complex of Guilt*

Matias resembles the archetypal literary outsider. Born in the customs house of a border station, the son of an immigrant, he possesses a foreign-sounding name; he thinks of himself as the one "who does not know the rules of the game."[6] A rootless individual, Matias has been in exile since the day of his birth and certainly is a version of the "stranger" figure characteristic of twentieth-century literature.[7] Matias deeply senses his loss of innocence, and his guilt over this feeds the guilt he feels for his later life. His need to regain psychological authenticity is linked to a desire to restore his spirit of childhood. The motorcycle accident for which he believes himself responsible may be, as Kjell Berger points out, an image of his internalized guilt for having killed the child within himself. He says: "There no longer is a child in the road, there are bloody clothes, there are intestines in the greasy dust, there is a rag doll with a screwed-on head, an astonished, undamaged head."[8] As we lose touch with childhood innocence, all that remains is the head—the arid, reasoning, intellectualizing part of ourselves. The child struck down in the road reminds one of the lifeless, mechanical doll in Wilfred Sagen's Paris studio. The unfinished sweater suggests that the child was destroyed before it had any opportunity to develop further. Thus Matias considers himself guilty of psychological and physical infanticide. But society denies him the right to conventional punishment. How can society do otherwise when nearly every adult member is equally guilty of murdering the child within himself? If society accepted Matias's confession of guilt, it would expose its own. All the episodes in *"Jeg"* are related, in one way or other, to the "accident." When the police declare that Matias is guilty of no crime, he tries to still his guilty conscience by turning to drink and women. The defense of Teodor, which he overhears by chance, infuriates him, because he sees the similarity between Teodor's case and his own. The arguments given to explain Teodor's crime— namely, the revelation of his unhappy childhood—and the attempts of the humanitarian to generate pity for the accused by underscoring his love of animals, are, to Matias, means of removing all responsibility from the individual. They are the moral judgments of the welfare state, denying the individual a basic, human right, namely the right of redemption through punishment. In his typically laconic way, Matias expresses his preference for the harsher values of another age: "I believe it is good for us to be punished," he says.[9]

In the conversation between Matias and Mrs. Skarseth the problem of guilt again comes into focus. Mrs. Skarseth's interminable babbling reveals her preoccupation with three things: her dead husband, her daughter Johanna, and Sonja. She betrays guilt for having wished her husband's death and above all for having denied Johanna maternal affection. She destroyed Johanna's childlike spontaneity and turned her into a hard and bitter woman. Like Matias, Mrs. Skarseth has committed infanticide.[10] But her chatter at least prepares Matias to attempt expiation by sharing knowledge of his torment with another. And this he will do by virtue of his confession to Sonja.

III   *Matias's Story*

Matias Roos is far more reluctant about relating the story of his past than Mrs. Skarseth has been with regard to her own. Before he met Sonja he apparently was tight-lipped. But Sonja is a trained psychologist, and he is in love with her. So she draws out of him the sources of his guilt feelings. At first Matias hesitates: "I cannot tell you this about myself because it no longer is me, it was part of the person who used the name with which I later became burdened. As far as I am concerned, [that person] is 'he.' His name was Matias Roos, he became known as such. His identity papers said so."[11] Once he begins to speak, however, Matias becomes wholly absorbed in his story. It clearly has a cathartic effect upon him. He tells Sonja about the people he once knew—most especially a mild, musical friend who perished by drowning, and a cynical opportunist who persuaded Matias to employ his skills in the manufacture of articles of destruction. These individuals, perhaps two sides of Matias himself, have represented stings of conscience for his loss of innocence, and the recollections of them would dredge up guilt feelings. Now, however, Matias relishes speaking about them. He is turning his past into a work of art. Matias's story has an expressionistic setting. He relates his visit to the inn Nobriskro and how he encountered there the shadows of all the important personalities from his past life. By turning the shattered fragments of his past into an esthetically satisfying whole, Matias senses the experience of creating form.

As he tells his story, the reader discovers that Matias is an artist. Society, like the gambling table he describes in the Nobiskro sequence, turns nearly all of us into losers. Only the cheaters win. In the background, however, detached from society's whirl but observing it in minute detail, stands the artist. Matias places such a character into his story. He makes of him a flute-player, a kind of Pan, the only figure in Nobiskro who has retained a link to childhood. Matias associates the flute-player with his childhood friend Fartein, who drowned in shallow water during a regatta many years earlier, because those who had seen him in trouble were too preoccupied competing with one another to come to his aid.[12] Fartein is a part of Matias, which he has lost and with which he wishes to reestablish contact. This would be Matias's chief aim in telling the story. Art, to be sure, never will restore him to permanent innocence, but at least it will put him into contact—however temporarily—with that innocent part of himself that he thought he had lost. By putting the fragments of his past into artistic order, Matias is able to gain perspective upon his life, and for a while liberate himself from his excruciating feelings of guilt.

The "he" in Matias's story is a fugitive in quest of a frontier that will bring his exile to a permanent end. Matias himself doubts whether the frontier will ever be found. What he finds is a point at which he could stop, look back, and perceive what led him there. Though he has not yet attained the blessed frontier that will restore all innocence and dissolve all guilt, Matias at least has reached the point of creating form out of his torment. He reveals to Sonja how, as a gifted chemist, he sold his technical skills to the highest bidder and thus contributed to war and death. He tells how he became involved in political terrorism. But his guilt does not stem originally from his supposed crimes against society. Its source is psycho-

logical, arising from consciousness of his split personality.
Matias senses that he must delve deeply into his past to get
to the root of his schizophrenia. Internal voices encourage him
to try. This leads him to an episode from his childhood, the
episode of the English chair. Relating it offers Matias the
psychoanalytical therapy that liberates him, for the moment,
from his neurosis.

For Matias the episode of the English chair was clearly the
climactic event of his childhood. So important is it that Matias
subconsciously switches persons in his story, referring to himself
as "I" and not "he." The change in pronoun suggests that Matias
has attained contact with the identity he thought he had lost
forever. The actual chair was an old piece of furniture that
Matias's parents had stored in an attic, mostly because it evoked
sinister connotations.[13] As Matias learned later, his great-
grandmother had died in it. For the fourteen-year-old boy and
his playmates the chair symbolized a taboo; it stood for a danger
which no one possessed the courage to confront. The supreme
feat of courage would have been to climb into the attic at
night and sit in the English chair. One day, feeling challenged
by the bravery of another boy, Matias decided that he would
perform the dreaded act. He told his friends in an almost
fatalistic way: "Tonight I shall sit in the English chair."[14] That
evening he crawled up to the attic, sat down in the chair, and
succumbed to a horrifying crisis. Like the boy who climbed
the honeysuckle vine, he fainted and ultimately was rescued
by his parents.

Later Matias begins to associate the strange incident of the
English chair with a change in his psychological development.
After the episode he felt that he had broken forever with the
protected, harmonious world of childhood. Actually the break
was nothing sudden. Matias had sensed it approaching for
several years. It provided a dramatic climax, as inevitable as
the explosion that follows upon the burning-down of a fuse
in a dynamite stick: "Perhaps the fuse had been lit for a long
time, but I had not noticed the fire—perhaps I had simply seen
it as tiny stings of desire and repulsion, like fire and ice."[15] A
compulsive need to compete and surpass other boys had prepared Matias for his break with childhood innocence. He

developed a sense of inadequacy, of insecurity. The shock Matias felt in the English chair symbolized his crossing of the frontier between the innocence of childhood and the exile of adolescence. The most immediate consequence is the break with his friend Fartein. The latter left Matias and later perished, a victim of the spirit of competition. Disappearing along with Fartein, of course, was Matias's own singing, childlike self, the side of his personality that he should have protected and preserved. Fartein was in happy harmony with nature: "Fartein could whistle like all the birds, they would come and sit on him."[16] Once he disappeared Matias became overwhelmed by fear and guilt. Only when he becomes an artist, a storyteller, can he reestablish contact with Fartein and by so doing cope with his anguish.

Following the chair episode Matias experienced life mainly as preparation for death: "I knew it then: to be an adult is to die; it was the timeless quality of the adult that took up residence within me, the adult's non-relationship to existence—his genuine fear of death, his fear of not being privy to the secret of the universe."[17] Following his descent from the attic Matias could no longer accept the human condition as a child might—on its own terms. He saw himself divorced from nature, not a part of it. He longed for and feared his return to nature, through death. Guilty of having lost his sense of living authentically, genuinely, Matias revolted against his human condition. From a fear of seeing himself destroyed he developed a desire to become an agent of destruction. He turned into a diabolical scientist, a traitor to humanity. He confesses his emotions to Sonja: "Oh to be the forces that governed and exploded. Creator and destroyer. God! God! Let me be all! Let me become God!"[18]

The explosions created by Matias the chemist parallel the explosions created by Wilfred Sagen, the artist. The creations of each reflect a cry of anguish, guilt, and revolt. Matias's life lost its sense of harmony. If he ever is to retrieve his peace of mind, he must retrace his path back beyond the frontier he crossed at the age of fourteen. He longs to see Eden again, to escape the Nobiskro of his soul, where he is nothing more than a restless shadow.

IV *The Return Home*

In retelling the incidents that split apart his self Matias achieved a kind of psychological healing. But liberation through art is not enough. He still believes that he must undergo physical punishment for the murder years ago of the child within him. When Johanna kills Sonja, Matias unexpectedly gains the opportunity to atone for the death of an innocent. On this occasion the police declare him guilty and he is sentenced to several years imprisonment. Upon his release he looks for Mrs. Skarseth and discovers the poignant scene of reconciliation between her and her granddaughter. The mood affects him deeply. It symbolizes a coming together of elements and a return to harmony. In Part III of the novel Matias decides to retrace his route back to the house he left (in Part I). Unobserved and weeping, he leaves Mrs. Skarseth and her granddaughter. On his .way back to his forest cabin he passes by the scene of his "accident" four years earlier. He thinks of the chair and the knitting, but no longer feels guilt.

The conclusion of *"Jeg"* contains a certain sense of ambiguity. As he approaches the house in the forest, Matias is physically exhausted. He literally crawls to his doorstep. Contrasting with this mood is one in which nature seems to ring out a triumphant welcome for him. The evening air is warm and clean; birds sing; the movement of a fish in water causes a lake to sparkle with color: "Do you see him? Do *you* see him? Straws are nodding, straws bend over to ask. Spruces tingle gently. Soon here will be peace."[19] "I"—sensing reunion at last—encourages "he" to continue. However, the voice of a skeptic sounds a loud, discordant note—the voice of an individual who had advised Matias that journeys do not pay. And Matias tells himself: "One *can* redeem, but one does not thereby become free, one does not become a child again. One can only walk. That is all one can do. But one does not get anywhere. There is no frontier."[20] In short, then, it might be possible to reestablish, through art, a line of communication with one's lost self; but *permanent* repossession of the innocence of childhood, a *permanent* liberation from adult guilt—these can never be.

Nevertheless, the Matias who returns home is different from

the one who left the house in the forest four years earlier. The critic Kjell Heggelund notes the difference between Matias's boundless longing and limited achievement.[21] The innocence of childhood and union with the cosmos elude him, it is true; but Matias does find peace of mind at last. He fails to cross a mystical frontier, but succeeds in transforming his longing into a story—the esthetic recreation of his past. What he discovers is a compromise, life's consolation prize: "No man becomes a child again, nobody becomes whole; one may approach one's I and diminish the tension, convert it from the intolerable to the tolerable—and live on. That is all."[22]

Matias Roos, then, fails to cross the frontier that separates him from the "place" of authenticity. His longing was boundless, but the novel's form is circular. At the conclusion of *"Jeg"* Matias is exactly at the spot from where he began his journey. The house does not represent the ultimate goal, but rather a kind of refuge equivalent to Mrs. Frisaksen's cabin. Physically as well, Matias's house resembles that of the recluse in the *Lillelord* trilogy. In both cases Borgen stresses the closeness to water, a boat, a fishing net, and the gray wood shining through the peeling, red paint. It offers Matias freedom from the folly of society, but supplies no magic key to cosmic union. Earlier, in a conversation with Sonja, Matias explained that the forest and house once had been his last resort. At the novel's conclusion he confirms this view. Now that he has expiated his guilt through confession and punishment, the house offers Matias the opportunity to live out a resigned, solitary existence. Near the novel's conclusion the dialogue between "I" and "he" underscores this mood: "I say in him that actions lead to all evil. He responds with Sonja's words from that time: So one ought to place one's hands in his lap—? And I again answer him with his own words: why not, that is a good place for hands."[23]

In *"Jeg"* there are indications that Matias had undertaken similar journeys in the past and may well be forced to undertake others in the future. We can assume that the tension between "I" and "he" will start building up again, and that whenever this tension becomes intolerable, Matias will once more leave his house. As an old man now, the promise of death—Wilfred Sagen's ultimate option—offers him little hope of release. He addresses himself: "You probably do not even believe in death. Perhaps it is because you—the skeptic—believe in eternal life, not as hope but in fear."[24]

The conclusion of "*Jeg*" seems to indicate that in approaching the problem of human identity Borgen was moving away from the mystical tone of some of the short stories and the despair of *Lillelord*. He appeared to be heading toward a "resolution" based upon the individual's social withdrawal and his concentration upon artistic creativity. At the end of the novel, Matias knows that a dissolution in death will not solve his problem. He also knows that withdrawal alone will not bring him the peace of mind for which he is longing. Of more hope is his ability to transform his anguish into artistic images. Matias does not need to carry a copy of *Pan* in his pocket, because he has learned how to create his own flute-player. It is characteristic that, while Matias's story seems strongly influenced by *The Trial*, Kafka is never mentioned by name. Just as Matias has absorbed the message of Hamsun, so he has integrated Kafka into his own artistic personality, and the story he tells will quite naturally contain echoes from the works which have served as his literary guides. Borgen rightly rejects the accusation made by certain reviewers that "*Jeg*" is a kind of pastiche of *The Trial*. Yet he freely acknowledges the influence of Hamsun and Kafka, and the allusions he makes to them are explicit enough to render name-dropping superfluous. Moreover, by illustrating how each work of art inevitably builds on a literary tradition, Hamsun and Kafka serve a distinct function in the novel. Borgen brilliantly integrates these writers into his own, personal vision of reality.

CHAPTER 7

The Hero as Jolly Joker

"*JEG*" is a tightly structured novel. Comprehension of its form is essential for a satisfactory understanding of its meaning. On the other hand, *Blåtind* seems extremely diffuse, at least at first reading. The plot appears to be complex, the relationships among the characters unnecessarily involved. Matias Roos controls the point of view in "*Jeg*." In *Blåtind* several characters vie with one another to express their points of view. "*Jeg*" is packed with monologues disguised as dialogues: *Blåtind* combines monologue and dialogue.

I   The Plot

The novel is framed around a scene in a railway station near a Norwegian ski resort. *Blåtind* opens and closes on the same scene: three people have brought to the station the corpse of a man, Peter Holmgren, who has perished from exposure in the snowy mountains. One of the three, a woman called Nathalie Graetz, will accompany the body aboard a train. The corpse is headed for burial in Peter's native country, Sweden. Nathalie is Peter's estranged wife. The train arrives, the body is taken to the baggage car, the woman bids farewell to one of her two companions, and takes her place in the passenger section. The train then departs, leaving Claes Hermelin and Ole Bakk on the station platform. *Blåtind's* two final chapters complete the information given in the opening scene, filling in all the details. Most of the intervening sections reflect conversations between Claes and Nathalie and the thoughts that flash through the minds of Peter and Nathalie. Borgen focuses upon the idea of departure. Nathalie clearly is leaving something behind, perhaps the country itself, perhaps Claes. The opening lines of the novel echo Nathalie's resolute "No!"—a rejection of the mountains and

the people on the station platform: " 'No!' she repeated. The train
pulled out of the station. She did not want to look out of the
compartment window. But she vaguely perceived Claes Hermelin's back, a broad, strong back."[1]

The purpose of the novel is to explain the events leading up
to Nathalie's departure. The countryside around the ski resort is
majestically covered with snow and mountains. The most inaccessible of the peaks is "Blåtind." Only one person claims ever
to have reached it. In the course of the novel several others
head for "Blåtind," presumably with the intention of conquering
it. But none ever succeeds, and from beginning to end the peak
remains a symbol of cold, virgin purity.

The inhabitants of the resort and Peter Holmgren are the
central characters of *Blåtind*. The executive manager and presumed owner, Ole Bakk, is a one-legged little man possessing
no authority. The individual who genuinely runs the place is
the reception clerk, Claes Hermelin, whose cosmopolitan air
and apparent self-confidence charm and puzzle the guests.
Gradually the reader learns that Claes has led a multifaceted
life. His background is Jewish, and he has changed his name
several times. In the novel itself he sometimes is referred to
as "Bill." He has been involved in fraudulent art sales. Claes
is an uprooted individual, at first lacking spiritual, social, or
national identity, and who ultimately adapts to the universe of
"Blåtind." Nathalie, a former painter, a Jewish refugee who
miraculously escaped the Nazi death camps, is hostess at the
resort. The character gallery of guests forms a kind of chorus
that comments upon the episodes occurring inside and outside
the lodge. The existence of a mysterious skier who leaves a
wide circle of tracks around the hotel, preoccupies everyone.
Since nobody actually has seen the skier except as a vague,
distant shape against the mountain backdrop, the stranger takes
on a mystical, almost mythic dimension. The reader links him
to the corpse at the beginning of the novel; and it becomes
increasingly clear that the skier indeed is Peter Holmgren, a
wealthy Swede who had helped rehabilitate and settle homeless
refugees after World War II. Through flashbacks we learn that
Peter had liberated and aided Nathalie, eventually marrying
her. For a time the couple settled in Copenhagen, where Peter

continued his work with displaced persons. But a feeling that he was denying her the opportunity to develop an integral personality provoked Nathalie into leaving Peter. Her departure aggrieved her husband so that he gave up his position and left Denmark. He lives a restless existence and by chance winds up as the lonely skier making his way through the mountains that surround Ole Bakk's resort hotel.

Peter literally haunts the people at the resort. Inside the hotel Claes tells Nathalie of his own past, and of his links to Peter. Ole, Claes, and Peter are cousins. As boys they used to spend their summers together at the Holmgren estate in Bohuslän, an area in southwestern Sweden. A strong, brilliant boy, Peter was the natural leader of the group. His obsession to prevail over the others in all competitive activity was a constant strain upon the friendship of the boys. Claes recalls a time when he, Peter, and Ole—at Peter's insistence—decided to leap off a very high cliff into the sea below. The first who was scheduled to jump, Ole, the smallest and weakest of the boys, astounded the other two by diving elegantly into the sea. Claes withdrew from the competition out of fear. Himself paralyzed with fright, Peter nevertheless refused to acknowledge his inferiority, plunged from the cliff, and hit the water with his stomach, nearly killing himself. The incident sears into the later lives of the three. From it Ole gains confidence in his abilities and becomes a courageous member of the Norwegian Resistance during the German occupation. On the other hand, humiliated and ashamed, Peter cultivates a hatred of his cousin and ulti- mately betrays Ole to the Nazis. Subjected to torture, Ole loses his memory and a leg. His will is shattered and it is in this mutilated state that we find him as owner of the ski resort. He is utterly dependent upon Claes who, as we learn, even furnished the money for the purchase of the resort.

Therefore, Peter Holmgren is the direct cause of Ole's misery; and one may presume that Peter's involvement in rehabilitating refugees after the war stems from an effort to redeem the guilt he has acquired from his betrayal of Ole. The departure of Nathalie represented another humiliation for Peter. It thrust him into a spiritual vacuum, a mental state symbolized by his circumlocutions around the hotel.

A fire at the hotel introduces the climax of *Blåtind*. While burning down part of the resort, the conflagration has a cathartic effect upon Ole, Claes, and Nathalie. Peter, watching the blaze from afar, perishes in the cold and the snow. His body is recovered and brought to the hotel. Ole regains his memory and will. Claes realizes that he belongs to the country of "Blåtind," while Nathalie discovers that her place is elsewhere. Ultimately, Claes is left with regrets at the station platform, while Nathalie, in search of liberty and self-realization, parts with Peter's body.

II *Scandinavia and Europe*

On one level *Blåtind* may be read as a symbolic novel illustrating the ambivalent relationship between the Scandinavian countries and the rest of the continent. The temporal framework is postwar Europe, still living under the shadow of national betrayals and the death camps. Torn from its isolation, provincialism, and traditions of self-serving neutrality, the North still cannot adjust to the fact that the war has thrust it into the maelstrom of Europe. Among the Scandinavian countries themselves Denmark and Sweden are more "European" than rural, poor Norway. Claes and Peter are by birth Swedes, far more cosmopolitan in outlook and attitude than their little Norwegian cousin Ole. Claes is a Jew, son of a diplomat, and has spent a large part of his life abroad. Peter devotes himself to repatriating and aiding displaced persons from all corners of Europe. On the other hand, Ole got his first taste of European life from the inside of a German concentration camp.

In Peter Holmgren's betrayal of Ole Bakk, Borgen may be making a thinly veiled attempt to illustrate the displeasure of his countrymen over the Swedish decision, in 1940, to permit the Germans, following the invasion, to shuttle troops between Norway and Germany. For years after World War II Norwegian public opinion remained embittered over this. Yet it is Ole, rather than Claes or Peter, who prevails at the conclusion of the novel. Nevertheless, while far from united among themselves and possessing in varying degrees a sense of cosmopolitanism, Claes, Peter, and Ole represent a single family. They spring from a common source and offer a united front to the world beyond. On the station platform Claes lies down beside Peter's corpse. His Jewishness, which for a time pulled him toward the continent and England, disappears; and he settles forever in the country of "Blåtind."

Thus the three cousins seem to embody Scandinavian identity. Nathalie Graetz, on the other hand, is the perpetual refugee, a homeless wanderer. At a point in the novel each cousin tries to absorb her; but she resists, firmly insisting upon her intention to construct and retain an identity of her own choosing. Ultimately she leaves the country of "Blåtind." Where will she go? Borgen does not say. But Claes suggests that she will return to her art and in it find her way.

Borgen seems torn between the viewpoint of Nathalie and that of the cousins. In *Blåtind* he is critical of "the Scandinavian way of life." He represents the North's postwar humanitarianism as a conscience-salving effort to erase old feelings of guilt. While he does not define clearly the reasons for this guilt, one may surmise that it is related to the profiteering of the First World War that he described in such harsh terms in the *Lillelord* trilogy. What the Scandinavians prefer is to sink into a renewed stage of self-centered isolationism. Borgen contrasts Nathalie's courage and pragmatism with the inability of the male Scandinavians she knows to cope with reality. A morbid fear of losing out in competition with others paralyzes them. While the cousins compensate for their insecurities by contemplating an unattainable victory over "Blåtind," Nathalie makes her irrevocable decision to leave the North. While waiting for the train at the station, she tells herself: "I do not belong with them and their vague longings. I am not one of Blåtind's people."[2] Yet she leaves with regret, and, having witnessed Claes's demonstration of loyalty with the dead Peter, she is convinced that he has acted in accordance with the best forces within himself.

III *The Characters*

A commentary on the "Scandinavian condition" is merely one of several possible interpretations of *Blåtind*. An evaluation of the relationships among the characters offers additional insight into the novel. The characters may be distinguished as

the hotel guests, the triangle of Peter, Claes, and Ole, and
Nathalie Graetz. The fact that Nathalie forms an entity unto
herself emphasizes her importance. The hotel guests in *Blåtind*
form a choral backdrop of chatterers. They comment upon the
presence of the mysterious skier, gossip about the main characters, illustrate the cares and prejudices of their countrymen, and
on occasion sally forth in futile efforts to reach "Blåtind." Borgen
reports their conversations in fragments and scraps. The guests
are, for the most part, a bored lot; their ski excursions customarily
are brief. For them the most significant event of the season
is the hotel fire, a welcome break in their daily routine.

It is interesting to note the development of Peter, Claes, and
Ole from the Wilfred, Moritz, Birger triad of the *Lillelord*
trilogy. Just as Moritz represented Wilfred's double, so too does
Peter turn into a mirror image for Claes. Just as Birger became
the victim of Wilfred, so too does Ole become the victim of
Peter. For the three cousins the common point of departure
are the summers they spent as boys in Bohuslän. Ole was made
to sense his inferiority. He was a less proficient athlete than
either Claes or Peter, and he came from a poor Norwegian
branch of the family. Peter and Claes dominated him, but Ole,
who lacked personal ambition, did not seem to care. The two
Swedish cousins themselves were greatly unlike one another.
Claes was easygoing, but Peter was totally obsessed with a fear
of being outdistanced by him. Peter usually triumphs over the
other boys, but his victories leave a bitter taste. For example,
on one occasion the three participate in a grueling, circular
long-distance race. Claes and Ole drop out; but Peter drives
himself on, only to discover that no one is present to witness
his victory. Peter's fears of losing to Claes eventually overwhelm him, and he decides to escape his predicament by adopt-
ing his cousin's personality. He wishes to absorb Claes's social
ease and self-confidence. But, as we learn shortly thereafter,
Claes has his own identity problem.

Prior to the outbreak of World War II, Claes is an art student in Paris, then in London. After the German invasion he
starts working for the Norwegian government-in-exile. One day
he is asked if he can identify the photograph of an individual
suspected of collaborating with the Nazis. The photograph is

Peter's. Claes denies any knowledge of the person whose image is placed before him; but from this moment on he senses a loss of his own authenticity. When he learns that under torture Peter has given Ole's name to the Germans, all the suppressed hatred he had felt for his cousin starts to surface. His thoughts circle around the memory of the summers in Bohuslän. Why Ole's name? he keeps asking himself. He feels that he himself has been poisoned by Peter's morbid jealousy, and, by refusing to identify his cousin's photograph, he has in fact become an accomplice in Peter's "crime" against Ole Bakk. Claes feels that Peter has robbed him of his authentic personality; instead of being himself, he has become a counterfeit of his despised cousin. He even takes on a job that conforms to his psychological state. He discovers that he has a talent for counterfeiting art treasures and does so well that he passes off his creations as originals on the black market. Eventually, however, the degradation of his personality becomes unbearable, and he decides to embark upon a quest for authenticity. The war ends, and Claes eventually goes to Copenhagen, perhaps in the hope of divesting himself of his criminal avocation. It is on a trip to the waterfront where he intends to toss away one of his "masterpieces" that he encounters Nathalie Graetz. Subsequently he goes to Norway, finds Ole Bakk, and sets up his cousin as executive manager of the hotel. This, Claes hopes, will serve to redeem him from the guilt he feels toward Ole. But Claes never can free himself of the hold he believes Peter has over him. At the conclusion of *Blåtind* he lies down on the sled that is bearing Peter's body to the train. At this point the union between the two seems stronger than ever. One may say that Peter will continue to live as part of Claes.

It is clear that Peter Holmgren is the motor force in the triangle that includes Claes and Ole. Either directly or indirectly, it is Peter who provokes the main action in the novel. Peter's obsession with losing has put an end to the summers in Bohuslän; Peter is to blame for Ole's misfortunes; without direct knowledge of it he is the cause of Claes's identity crisis. In a quest for redemption he enters into refugee work, meets Nathalie Graetz, and tries to rehabilitate her. He marries her in order to award her an identity—the supreme sacrifice, he believes. But

Nathalie cannot tolerate his shadow over her. She rejects being
used by Peter for his *own* rehabilitation. She leaves him and
throws *him* into an identity crisis, one which ultimately leads
to his death.

It is clear that each member of the male triad in *Blåtind* has
lost his original personality—Ole in the Nazi torture chambers,
Claes under the self-imposed "influence" of Peter, and Peter
in his boyhood attempts to become Claes. Nathalie also has lost
hers. Like Ole she is a victim of the war. Nathalie's origins are
shadowy. She speaks French, she painted in the camp, she seems
to have been a Belgian Jew. When she encounters Peter, however, she has a sensation of being Nobody. She has neither
family nor friends, and lacks even a registration number. Her
past consists of seemingly unrelated fragments, and she is unable
to decide whether these are real or purely imaginary. Even her
surname is one that has been arbitrarily given to her. Nathalie's
rehabilitation proves to be very difficult, and Peter desperately
wishes to become her savior. In reality he is anxious to mold her
according to his own will. At this point Nathalie's consciousness reawakens and she comes to realize that Peter wishes to
deprive her of an elemental human right—that of forging her
own personality. After Peter marries her she fears sitting down
in the chairs he has bought for their apartment in Copenhagen.
To her they represent a net that she instinctively must avoid:

I had never sat in them, only tried out how it felt. They frightened
me. One sank into them. They caught you and didn't let go. As soon
as they first arrived I sat down in one of the comfortable chairs for
a few seconds—and thought: if you don't get up from here, you will
be seized by one of those hysterical paralyses, you will not *be able* to
get up, because you will not *want to*. I have seen men sink into
that type of chair and remain there; never women, though, they
only pretended—pretended it was comfortable.[3]

Nathalie rejects the temptation of becoming the creature of
Peter's design. She leaves him. Originally, Peter had expressed
a desire to help Nathalie restore her personality. His job as
restorer of physically and psychologically mutilated humans is
analogous to Claes's original profession as restorer of art treasures. Like Claes he finds that his true talent lies in the creation

of a counterfeit that he passes off as the real thing. It is interesting to notice that the "counterfeit" painting Claes wanted to throw into the sea was not a Van Gogh as we had originally been led to believe, but a portrait of Nathalie. Having learned about the girl from his cousin, Claes had painted an image of her based wholly upon his own imagination. Unlike Peter, however, Claes realizes that the painting is unrepresentative and throws it into the sea. Peter, on the other hand, refuses to admit that his "image" of Nathalie is false, and therefore denies her the opportunity to recover the personality she once had possessed. Nathalie, however, refuses to be Peter's reproduction of the human being she had the potential of becoming. She longs for her authentic self.

Despite *Blåtind's* complicated subplots the central theme of the novel is the struggle between Nathalie and Peter. From the initial meeting between the two the tension is evident. Physically exhausted and psychologically maimed, she emerges from the concentration camp barracks to find Peter seated at the registration table in the courtyard:

And as I stepped out of the darkened building, out into the moonlight floating over an earth that once had been, I then believed—no, I knew—that this was what was to come after the end. All the screams were silenced, all vision and visions, it finally was over, and the courtyard was bathed in a cold blue light, and over by the small table sat a man smoking his pipe; I was led towards him, I floated on the moonlight, it carried me towards the smell from the pipe and I asked for permission to say something, but the smoke from his pipe numbed me and lifted me into a state of euphoria and he asked about things and learned that I was nobody and that nobody was expecting me.[4]

At this point it seems that it will be far easier for Peter to mold Nathalie according to his design for her than for her to call up sufficient reserves of strength to restore a shattered personality. The moonlight, the silence, and the aroma of his pipe smoke contribute to the pleasure she feels in simply being absorbed by him. Even in her weakened state, however, Nathalie does display an element of will. She asks to speak, to exert her human right to a point of view denied her during her incarceration in the camp. Her need to speak develops into a verbal defense against Peter. This is illustrated by her remarks in the opening pages of the novel, as the train carrying her and Peter's body leaves the station: "Personally I believe it is the obvious right of a fugitive to have her story heard; I know my story will be constructed of blocks that appear to contradict each other. However, I must have the right to defend myself against Peter Holmgren, he was the one who always was right. And his power to be heard extends beyond death."[5]

As long as they remained together, Nathalie and Peter struggled with one another for the right to speak. For Peter it was the extension of his earlier rivalries with Claes and Ole. Once he decides upon molding Nathalie it appears to be no contest. He is handsome, healthy, young, rich, and intelligent. She is a physical and mental wreck, and her social identity has been all but wiped out. But Peter's strengths prove deceptive. That he will lose becomes evident from the role Borgen assigns him in the novel. As *Blåtind* opens he is a corpse. In the flashbacks his point of view prevails only on two occasions, for a total of thirty-six pages.[6] Most of the remainder of the novel is seen through the eyes of either Nathalie or Claes. Claes's point of view is expressed in the stories he tells Nathalie. Peter's presence is as a specter that haunts the other characters. He prevails over Claes, but not over Nathalie. At the conclusion of *Blåtind* Claes expresses his certainty that Nathalie may well crown her victory over Peter by regaining her authentic self.

IV   *Peter's Circles*

At the source of Peter's problem is his egoism, based on a morbid fear of losing and a need to have others recognize his superiority. When Nathalie leaves him he is jolted out of his customary psychological state, senses his unauthenticity, and considers himself a "jolly joker" miming a human being. He undergoes a crisis but dies just as he is on the verge of resolving it. In the novel Peter is frequently seen moving around in physical and psychological circles. Borgen repeatedly stresses the circular pattern of his life. As a young boy, he once found himself wishing to pass a stationary horse. The animal instinctively tried to prevent this. Peter insisted. Soon he and the horse were engaged in a ridiculous charade. Peter's reason for wanting to pass the horse was based upon fear—fear of being kicked by the animal. It was a groundless fear, analogous to his obsession of being destroyed if he does not prevail in all he attempts to do. The horse symbolizes the omnipresent adversary in Peter's existence. In his escapade with the animal he eventually sank to the ground in exhaustion. Far from admitting defeat, however, he returned to the creature the next day, climbed upon its back, and taught himself to ride—that is, tame—it.

Peter's need to excel over others extends to acts of sadistic bravado. One day he apparently entered the python's cage in the Copenhagen zoo, killed the reptile, and mutilated its body in order to outperform Claes, who previously had killed and cut up a viper discovered by the pair along a forest path. For Peter possession of Nathalie represented the possibility of a supreme achievement. But Nathalie's moral strength lay in inverse proportion to her physical weakness, and she successfully resisted Peter's efforts to mold her personality. She threw Peter into a spiritual vacuum. He felt a need to escape from human contacts and rediscover a sense of authenticity. His subsequent arrival as the mysterious skier circling in wide swaths around Ole's hotel illustrates his mental state. Nathalie's resistance defeated him, but it was a defeat sustained by an unauthentic self. Where is he to turn now?

Both physically and mentally Peter is lost and wishes to find a steady course again. As is customary with him, he thinks he can locate it through a superhuman physical act, the conquest of an overpowering mountain peak. "Blåtind," with its associations of purity and solitude, defies him, and Peter insists upon taming it. This time he will do it alone, with no one's assistance, without even a witness. Equipped with a map, a compass, and a watch, he tries to orient himself in space and time. His map, however, does not accord with the landscape he observes in front of him, the time indicated by his watch does not fit the place of the sun in the sky. The compass is pointing him in a direction that his eyes tell him is obviously wrong. The map, the watch, and the compass, instruments in which Peter had believed he could have confidence, fail him when he needs them most. They lead him in circles, and he can only hope to get back on course with the help of his own eyes.

It is tempting to compare Peter's quest for "Blåtind" with Wilfred's quest for solitude. Wilfred was guided by two beacons: first, the volume of *Pan* which he used to carry in his pocket, second, the glass egg which he clutched in his hand when he died. Both these beacons pointed Wilfred away from an active existence and other people, toward passivity, solitude, and death. Only when it is too late to change course does Wilfred start suspecting that his beacons may have been misleading him. Peter's beacons are less literary, and the symbolism in his case is more subtle. His beacons are his instruments of orientation, and Peter hopes that they will guide him toward a goal. Instead they lead him onto a circular track, he loses touch with time and space, and he will surely perish if he continues to place his faith in them.

In addition to his map, watch, and compass, Peter has carried with him to the mountains a rich equipment of words and phrases. In his monologue he refers to himself as "a son of the mountains," his wandering is a "pilgrimage," he is longing for a "purifying bath" in the white snow, and he thinks of death as a "return to the womb of mother earth." Yet, just as he comes to realize that his map, watch, and compass are leading him astray, so does he discover that his verbal equipment can no longer be trusted. The phrases which should have given meaning to his undertaking are meaningless, empty clichés, and he himself is a clown, a jolly joker. Not knowing what to do, he nevertheless continues his wandering toward "Blåtind"—afraid of being lost, of freezing to death, of never arriving at his goal. Even his aim he eventually considers to be fruitless: "But then getting there is no goal either, for the day he is 'there'—what then?"[7] Still without responding adequately to his gnawing doubts, like a mole or a hibernating bear Peter will dig himself into his fur sleeping bag, swallow a dose of sleeping pills, and escape into the blessed state of unconsciousness. One evening, however, even his pills let him down. He wakes up abruptly in the middle of the night, crawls out of his hole, and is seized by a sensation of being in a void: "No storm. Nothing. The thought struck him: *Nothing*."[8] Fear keeps him from reentering the cave, or "grave" as he now calls it, he puts on his skis and his rucksack, and starts advancing in the darkness. In this moment a new, enormous beacon unexpectedly lights up before his eyes. In the distance Peter discovers the flames from the blaze at Ole's hotel, and realizes that his whole trek toward the summit of the mountain had been a mistake: "He thought: if only I can get there.—To Blåtind?—No, to human beings, to people. His voice came back and he finally said it out loud: 'If only I can get back to people!' Then he dozed off a little."[9]

Without knowing it Peter had been circling around his own past. Down below are the three individuals who had played such important roles in his previous existence—namely, Claes, Ole, and Nathalie. Peter was searching for the inevitable frontier that would lead him to purity and psychological authenticity. The pattern he wove with his skis was the same as the pattern he was weaving in his mind. The goal never came closer, and Peter had a gnawing suspicion that the goal itself was meaningless. Peter's journey toward the chilly whiteness of "Blåtind," away from civilization and its imperfections, was, in effect, one last cliché in a life that had become a parody of itself. Since Nathalie's departure Peter no longer was able to take himself seriously. In his ultimate journey he played one final part: that of the joker.

At the conclusion of their wanderings, Wilfred Sagen and Matias Roos discovered two different sorts of liberation. Wilfred found the peace of death, and Matias obtained a catharsis through confession and resignation. Both were conscious of what was happening to them and accepted it. Peter's last moments are far more pathetic than theirs. Unable to walk any further, he sinks into the snow again, mistakenly believing that he has successfully returned to human beings. Peter perishes because he is not alert enough. Instead of shaking off his drowsiness and continuing his walk in the direction of the hotel, he pulls out his brandy bottle and abandons himself to his last fantasy. Peter dies humming a tune: "'They did not know me,' he said. He said it several times, with stiff lips. He wanted to say more, tell them everything. But the teeth were bolted together, the jaw locked. So he could only hum. He felt the summer night round him now—a gaiety. He hummed to madam, got up humming. He hummed about the jolly jokers. . . . Then he fell. He saw the smoke but no longer had any thoughts about it. Then he hummed no more."[10]

A certain sense of mirth precedes Peter's death. Wilfred felt joyful as well. In Wilfred's case, however, the happiness was genuine. He enjoyed a sense of legitimate release. Peter's mirth is filled with self-deception and self-mockery; it is built upon frustration and failure. He acknowledges his role as the deck's jolly joker, at the moment of death humming his problems away. In fact, Peter is not really aware of his own death. He never does relate his complete story. He never does maintain his right to speak. Having yearned for the bliss of solitude, he finds only freezing silence. Seeing the fire below, sensing the presence of humanity there, he starts longing to escape from the circular track that imprisons him. He wants to reach people and tell them what he himself has so painfully learned. But his body and will betray him, and his jaw is brutally locked. He cannot even communicate any longer with the mountains.

During the two final chapters of *Blåtind* Peter is physically present only as a corpse. One of the guests finds his body, and Claes brings it back to the hotel. Ole, Claes, and Nathalie have it transported to the nearest railway station. Nathalie will accompany the body on the train. Her departure represents her resounding repudiation of enslavement to the vague longings of "Blåtind's" people. Her decision to leave for good becomes firm when she witnesses Claes lying down next to the corpse on the sled.[11] Her relationship to Peter now assumes a wholly practical aspect. She will take care of the details of burying him. Assuming responsibility for Peter's body, she is freed from what she believes to be his spiritual heritage. The same, however, cannot be said for Ole and Claes. Peter, whose role in the novel is literally that of a dead weight, will continue to haunt them. Ole and Claes will remain "the people of Blåtind," chained to the past, to Peter's vague longings for absolute purity, for innocence. Ironically, they will never know what Peter's experience had taught him. The ghost is completely shut off from conveying his final message to them. They will therefore wither away in their circular reverie, while Nathalie will break out of the circle through activity that will conform with her authentic self. Claes predicts as much: "She will paint again, she will be happy, she is the one among us who became whole, innocent."[12]

The conclusion of *Blåtind* therefore represents a marked departure from that of the *Lillelord* trilogy and "*Jeg.*" Nathalie's "No" to a life of passivity, resignation, and search for absolutes is the obverse of the submissive attitudes of Miriam and Sonja. When Wilfred saw Miriam for the last time before his death, she was like a lamp, "her face was illuminated from within."[13] Yet Wilfred knows that it is too late for him to change course. The light that Peter sees is much more violent, and he is confident that the new beacon will lead him back to human reality. It is the irony of life (as well as of the author) that denies him the opportunity of a fresh start.

Even more pathetic than Peter at the end of the novel is Claes. Earlier he had hated Peter, accusing his cousin of draining his strength away in vampirelike fashion. At the end Claes himself is the vampire, attempting to suck spiritual force from a corpse. Instead of searching for a way to build an authentic existence for himself, he will live on as a counterfeit of his cousin. He has become a falsifier in a profound sense. Worst of all, Claes never knew Peter deeply enough to share his cousin's experience of enlightenment. The image of Peter that Claes carries in his mind is as far removed from reality as the picture he had once painted of Nathalie. Nathalie's picture he threw into the sea, while the false image of Peter will become the beacon that will guide him through life.

CHAPTER 8

Myth–Its Rewards and Limitations

*B*LÅTIND departs from Borgen's earlier novels in at least one significant way. The character whose point of view prevails is not a cerebral, complex male but rather a simple, direct, pragmatic female. Nathalie's elemental need to express herself is the consequence of a lengthy, forced suppression of her will. Her point of view is strengthened by Peter's pathetic defeat in the snow. In *Blåtind* the simple character is the stronger. One never doubts Nathalie's ability to bury Peter and the past and rebuild her existence according to her authentic wishes.

In *Den røde tåken* (1967), Borgen reestablishes his focus upon the complex male and his point of view. The only female of any significance, the girl Lillegull, is hardly more than a child. Murdered by the protagonist when he himself was in his teens, she also is a literary scapegoat. Lillegull is defenseless and pitiful. But it is not merely restoration of a male point of view that marks Borgen's transition from *Blåtind* to *Den røde tåken*. The later novel's most noticeable characteristic is its airtight compactness. It represents an important departure from *Blåtind*'s rambling structure.

The root themes of *Den røde tåken* are familiar ones: crime and punishment, fall and redemption. What predominate are the novel's remarkable structural unity and a welcome quality of lyricism that the author achieved in his best short stories. Borgen confesses that he has thought of *Den røde tåken* as a piece of music.[1] Certainly the success of the novel is related to its form. The initial impression left is that of a direct and uncomplicated work. But this is a deceptive view. The novel is rich in allusive qualities, that strike the reader only in gradual fashion. The critic Kjell Heggelund found *"Jeg"* operating

112

within the framework of *The Trial* and *Peer Gynt*. *Den røde
tåken* brings to mind the Old Testament, Greek mythology,
and certain themes of Kierkegaard and Ibsen. These allusions
serve the essential idea of climb and fall, liberty and death.
Furthermore, Borgen awards centrality of place to architecture
and sculpture, suggesting that he again is probing into the
role of art as a means of helping to resolve the protagonist's
identity problem.

I *The Plot*

Externally, *Den røde tåken* resembles a Greek tragedy. The
novel describes less than thirty-six hours in the life of the
protagonist, the period that preceded his climactic "awakening."
Scattered flashbacks in memory serve as a chorus. They bring
to mind incidents and crimes for which he has served a lifetime
of guilt. A hotel and park, each within walking distance of the
other, delimit the novel's frame. Such a classical use of time
and space successfully raises Borgen's story above its contemporary setting and gives it a universal dimension.

The central character of *Den røde tåken* is anonymous, and
the town where the plot unfolds is known simply as "X-by," i.e.,
Norwegian for "X-town." On an October evening the protagonist
returns to the town where he had spent his boyhood. His
behavior suggests that he is hiding from justice. His extraordinary height preoccupies him. Though he is virtually blind
without his spectacles, he removes them. He nervously scru-
tinizes newspaper headlines and wonders whether those individuals he encounters will later recognize him. Flashbacks running
through his mind make it clear that his fears are intimately
connected with a series of incidents that had occurred many
years before.

The first incident surrounded a cruel childhood prank. At
the age of twelve he one day had accepted the challenge of
his friend and rival, Herman. He climbed a tall tree and
destroyed the eggs that a pair of kingfishers had left in their
nest. A second incident had more serious ramifications. A year
after the scene with the kingfishers, in a fit of rage, the protagonist had attempted to kill Herman. The two were leaning

over a lake not far from the tree the boy had previously climbed. The protagonist grasped Herman's head, plunged it into the water, and would have held it there had not the screams of a frightened duck distracted him. He loosened his hold and Herman escaped. Ultimately the protagonist had another chance at Herman, did murder him, and it is for this crime that he has been imprisoned.

But it is not responsibility for Herman's death that plagues him to the point of escaping from prison and running back to "X-by." Very early in *Den røde tåken* Borgen introduces a newspaper clipping that refers to an unsolved mystery concerning a young girl. This is Lillegull. A resident of "X-by," she vanished one day and was presumed murdered. But a police investigation failed to uncover either her body or the mystery surrounding her disappearance. Fragments passing through the mind of the protagonist reveal an intimate youthful relationship between himself and Lillegull. When the two were fourteen, he loved her ardently. She embodied his adolescent idea of purity. But Herman made a shambles of this image and provoked him into committing the crime that has stalked him all his life. Herman challenged the protagonist into watching him seduce Lillegull in a tool shed near the spot where the kingfishers' nest had been sacked. The newpaper article, subsequent flashbacks, and the protagonist's peculiar behavior after running back to "X-by" make it evident that he bears a certain responsibility for Lillegull's disappearance; and it is guilt over this that is tearing him. Not until the final pages of the novel, however, is he able to clarify his relationship to the girl, face up to the crime he has committed at her expense, and atone for it.

On returning to "X-by" remnants from the past swarm through the protagonist's mind. He settles down for the night in the town's most comfortable hotel, eats his evening meal, takes a bath, swallows a couple of sleeping pills, and falls into an uncomfortable, broken sleep. His dreams and thoughts center upon Herman and Lillegull. He rises early the following morning and ruminates for several hours over his personal history. Then, armed with a collection of tourist brochures, he leaves the hotel and heads out of town. At the edge of "X-by" a park has been built. In the center of it the citizens have erected a 750-foot monolith dedicated to the spirit of liberty. The protagonist arrives at the gigantic monolith and begins to climb it. Figures carved into the structure, intended to represent mankind's progress toward freedom, serve as his staircase upward. Despite his excruciating experience the protagonist is undaunted and arrives at his goal, a lion of stone which crowns the monolith. He confronts the sculpture for a few seconds and then leaps to his death. During his fall the details surrounding Lillegull's disappearance surface in his consciousness. Having witnessed her with Herman in the shed, he had rushed from his hiding place brandishing a knife, and attacked the couple. In his frenzy he killed Lillegull and buried her body not far from the shed. The police never found the corpse, but many years later the town fathers coincidentally built their monolith at the site where the shed once had stood. The protagonist's descent from the structure is intended as a coming to terms with his crime. His self-confession represents an expiatory act. His flight from the memory of Lillegull's death is over, and his fall toward her concealed tomb represents a unification of sorts, though Borgen undermines the Romantic conclusion with a measure of savage irony.

Den røde tåken is not a realistic novel but an allegory. The plot is very simple and all the dimensions in the novel are exaggerated. The climb to the top of the gigantic monolith is a superhuman act, and must be seen as a mental rather than a physical feat. The murder of Lillegull can perhaps be seen in this way as well. It may be interpreted as an extended version of the youthful prank against the kingfishers' nest.

II *Alienation and the Fall from Innocence*

At its most basic level *Den røde tåken* concerns a criminal's return to the scene of his crime and his effort to cope with past guilt. Throughout the novel, but especially during the fall from the monolith, which Borgen describes in a camera sequence of very slow motion, patches of the protagonist's life invade his consciousness. The episodes are fragmented, but form the raw matter of a chronology. They permit a reconstruction of the protagonist's past, allowing himself and the reader to focus upon those episodes that were to mark him significantly. All relate to the problems of alienation and guilt over a fall from innocence.

The first episode occurs forty years in the past. A flash of involuntary memory restores to consciousness the protagonist's childhood home. In a manner recalling Proust's, a scent in the park near the monolith evokes the fragrance of the garden that once had surrounded his parents' house:

Oh wonder: fragrance of lilacs in October! My mother—with her broadbeamed hat of yellow straw, with her knitting and mending basket, there she goes through the field scented with lilacs, and pungently intermingled with the aroma produced by gentlemen swiftly relieving themselves in the semidarkness of the garden pavilion, when the summer evening drinks tormented them and the sea patiently sighed beneath the cliffs and the cries of the terns ceased and all became silent until the prolonged, pained shrieks of the owls took possession of the night. And this is now. He stood perfectly still and knew that in the course of a second or less nearly forty years had collapsed inside him.[2]

The flashback introduces a well-to-do bourgeois household, where refreshments in the garden formed part of the late afternoon routine. The image of the mother, associated with the fragrance of the flowers, evokes the childhood Eden, where peace, warmth, and comfort reigned. It is the protagonist's Combray. But the idyll is coming to an end. The sea emits a sigh of weariness; the cries of the terns suddenly cease and are replaced by the pained shrieks of the owls. The description of his mother's garden presages the first crisis in the protagonist's life, the inevitable passage from childhood to adolescence.

Later in the novel another flashback places the protagonist, age twelve, on a deserted island. In this case a sense of smell links moments in the past to one another. The memory of an odor he associates with a trip to Italy evokes in his mind a very clear memory of his adventure on the island. The boy is lost. He has been rowing, "rowing away from all he loved"—and he disembarks on the island. It is a windswept place, "without trees or growth of any kind, only folds, deep as valleys, valleys in the shape of crevices—like a giant model of a brain. He got lost on that island and knew only a single fixed point: the crevice where his boat was tied."[3] In his exploration of the island the boy loses his way. Terrified, he passes an entire day wandering about, an intruder subject to the attacks of seabirds. At last he locates his boat and can begin his journey home. The boy's experience encapsulates his past and future. It symbolizes the voyage from the garden of childhood to the wasteland of adulthood, with the accompanying sense of guilt, self-betrayal, and loss. But it also bodes a certain hope of movement toward the haven left behind. What was lost is the opportunity to pass through life without falling from innocence. Borgen poses a question rather than expresses a fact: in life can one find his way back?

The brutal manner in which the protagonist has fallen from innocence, illustrated by the shattering opening scene in the novel, seems to convey a negative response to Borgen's question. The episode is the destruction of the kingfishers' eggs, as imprinted in the protagonist's memory. He and Herman stand beneath a tall tree where the nest is situated. They observe it. The two adult birds fly out in search of food, leaving the eggs untended. Herman defies his friend to climb the tree and destroy the eggs, in order to test the reactions of the kingfishers on their return. At first the boy hesitates, but then falls for the temptation to take up the challenge. Just as he throws the eggs to the ground, the peaceful evening is transformed into a tumult. The birds return to the nest and emit piercing shrieks of pain. Panicked, the protagonist loses his spectacles and chaos reigns. Before the climb all is harmony and beauty:

The promontory that penetrates into the shining sea. Reeds at sunset. At the extreme edge of the promontory the red pine tree, redder than usual now that the sun is sinking. Blue dragonflies low over the water. From the town distant church bells.[4]

Moments later the atmosphere has changed:

Leaned over the shelf with the nest, holding an egg in his hand. Let it drop to the ground. A scream from below. Held an egg in his hand once more. Madness. Good madness in the crotch. Sunset sparkling red flames, flaming sunset outside and within. In his eyes red flames. Hurled the egg into the rocks below. Red, red madness.

Hurled the third egg to the ground and sunset and birds screaming
and darkness and mother.
   "Someone is coming!"
Screaming birds above. Darkness below.
Slid down the trunk so fast that he skinned his legs.
   "My spectacles!"
Fog before his eyes. No red sky. "Where are you?"
Nothing. Fog.
   "My spectacles! Herman."
No one. Nothing. Stumbled blindly.
   "H e r m a n!"[5]

The episode with the kingfishers underscores betrayal on
several levels. The boys' prank betrays the nocturnal peace
of nature. In destroying the eggs they betray life itself. By running
off with his spectacles, thus leaving him helpless and alone in
the red fog of his blindness, Herman betrays his companion. The
fall from innocence leads inexorably to what will become the
cataclysmic act in the life of the protagonist: the murder of
Lillegull. This seems to occur approximately two years after the
experiences on the desert island and with the kingfishers' eggs.
Once again Herman is the tempter, provoking his friend into
performing a deed that not only certifies his loss of innocence
but also deepens his sense of alienation. For the protagonist,
Lillegull's murder is so horrible a crime that he is unable to confess it. He will try to push responsibility for it out of his consciousness. But the guilt haunts him without surcease, and his
life becomes a desperate search for an escape route, a means
of extricating himself from his tortured state of mind. At length
he appears to accept the fact that a possible way to secure
relief from his anguish would be by returning to its geographical
source. So he escapes from prison where he is serving a sentence
for the murder of Herman, and he runs back to the place where
his innocence originally was lost: to "X-by."

III   *The Double*

Herman's role in *Den røde tåken* is important but puzzling. In
the protagonist's mind he has no redeeming qualities. He is a
snake, a tempter. The protagonist despises him with all his

heart. Reflecting surfaces and the sound of water nearly always restore to consciousness the attempted drowning of Herman. During the evening the protagonist spends in his hotel room a vision of the episode reappears on several occasions:

Hears water bubbling from the bathtub and toilet bowl and is filled with warm well-being. The lake, the small lake encircled by reeds— suddenly he sees it before him. And Herman's head, Herman's reflection in the water before he grasped Herman's head, grasped his neck, and shattered the reflection of Herman's head with Herman's own head, Herman's head that he held under the water in a grip of steel round the neck.

Stands and watches the tub empty, sees the toilet bowl fill with clear, greenish water. Herman's head in the water.[6]

Far from evoking guilt or shame, the recollection of Herman's head in the water comforts the protagonist. His only regret seems to be that the murder was unsuccessful, that he had lacked the willpower to go through with it. He would have welcomed being judged for Herman's death. Furthermore, had Herman perished in the lake, the shed episode would never have taken place, and the "terrible act"—the murder of Lillegull—would have been avoided. The protagonist does not hesitate to consider Herman responsible for the girl's death: "I had in any case never said anything, not about the terrible [act], about his guilt, yes, his, not mine."[7]

Herman serves the function of a double for the protagonist, a cynical observer who undermines all the protagonist's feelings and acts. Of course, in his previous fiction Borgen utilized the device of the literary double—Wilfred-Moritz in *Vi har ham nå*, "I"-"he" in *"Jeg,"* Peter-Claes in *Blåtind*; and like so many of his predecessors, the protagonist of *Den røde tåken* is schizoid. Consciousness of his loss of innocence led to the shattering of his personality. And Herman, he felt, was the one who provoked the disintegration. Exposed to Herman during the crucial years of his adolescence, he had to accept his friend's challenges and commit acts that subsequently shamed himself. So profound did Herman's malevolent influence become that the protagonist started to look upon his companion as a part of his own personality, "all that dragged and pulled in a direction that I did not wish to go, where nobody wished to go—"[8] Therefore, in the scene beside the lake, when the protagonist bent over the water and discovered Herman's head reflected next to his own, he painfully experienced the division within his mind and heart. His desire to kill Herman represented a psychological need to be rid of the degraded part of the self. In accomplishing this the adolescent hoped to become complete and innocent once more.

The successful murder of Herman several years later, never fully described, fails to achieve its intended result. The double continues to reside within the protagonist. Whenever he sees or recalls a reflecting surface, Herman's face accompanies his own, and mocks him: "He bent down and *saw*, saw his own face, and then suddenly: Herman's face more deeply in the mirror."[9] "Bends once again toward the mirror and seeks out Herman's boneless face in his own bony one."[10] Herman has become a part of the protagonist that he refuses to accept. Since the protagonist's schizophrenia resulted from his loss of innocence, he surmises that reintegration of his personality will accompany his restoration to the garden. If he can find a means of confessing his guilt, perhaps he can expiate himself of it. Perhaps then he may attain a form of redemption, and with it the restoration of innocence and liberty. Perhaps then he will be free of Herman. Coming to terms with his past may heal his psyche.

IV   *The Monolith*

A loss of clear vision accompanied the protagonist's fall from innocence. His blindness was symbolically represented when, having ravaged the kingfishers' nest, the boy lost his spectacles and the red fog descended upon him. When he returns to "X-by," the protagonist still is myopic. His past comes back to him only in scattered fragments; his entire life appears dim and out of focus. Borgen's narrative devices—the use of a newspaper article, episodic descriptions of the protagonist's movements and thoughts as he enters "X-by," and of course the jumbled flashbacks—may illustrate broken vision. The devices stand in stark contrast to the near-classical unity of time and space in the novel. It is obvious that the quest for innocence and the quest for clear, comprehensive vision are intertwined. The protagonist cannot hope to redeem his guilt without first emerging from the dull red fog that engulfs his past.

The monolith that dominates the second half of the novel plays a vital role in the protagonist's quest. Receipt of the news of the monument's erection was what had led him to break out of prison and return to his home town. From tourist brochures he learns that the monolith is dedicated to freedom, and the protagonist assumes that it must possess the secret of liberation for himself as well. When he suspects that the structure has been raised on the site of Lillegull's murder, he becomes certain that it holds the answer he has been seeking; and so he becomes determined to find the monument and climb to its summit.

The way to the top is indeed a pilgrim's progress, since the climber must pass through each of the monolith's four sections. The bottom fringe contains carvings of prehistoric animals, presumably to remind man of his modest origins. Emerging from the fringe is a group of human bodies stretching upward, striving for material or spiritual goods. Then comes a section filled with inscriptions in large letters, meant to testify to the value of words. The next section represents a vacuum, perhaps the No-man's Land to which human effort eventually leads. Above this void is the topmost layer of the monument, which contains a group of individuals falling toward earth. Capping the entire structure is a lion of stone. The monolith suggests the process of life itself, with its ever-renewing cycle of birth, involvement in society, renunciation, and death. The townspeople of course are only observers, and witness the process from below. Because of a fog that covers the upper half of the monument, their vision is incomplete. They see clearly only the figures striving upwards. On the other hand, for the first time since his original fall, the protagonist—climbing steadily toward the summit—acquires a clear view of every stage of human existence, and ultimately, a comprehensive picture. At the top of the monument he witnesses the lifting of the fog. He has lost his spectacles again, but discovers that he no longer needs them. He beholds the lion, perhaps a symbol of divinity; but the creature tells him nothing. All is silent, all is clear. In the end true liberty consists of awareness of the futility of the struggle. A work of art has taught him this lesson. Ambition, striving, guilt—all active human emotions dissolve in the moment of total renunciation. Having seized his truth, the protagonist makes one final decision: he leaps from the monolith.

The protagonist's option of suicide is built upon a realization that all human activity leads to the inevitable fall. The vacuum on the monolith represents the futility of striving; and the plunging figures at the top of the structure emphasize the inevitable consequence of ambition, striving, and action. The protagonist never seems to weigh alternative options. He never even contemplates a way to descend alive. Life to him is synonymous with guilt, and he is tired of fleeing: *"The whole thing was a big mistake,"* he tells himself.[11] He has gained a comprehensive picture of life. He finds that the option he takes is the only one available. The liberty he hails is restricted indeed.

As the protagonist falls he unexpectedly gains an instant of contemplation that restores to him the spiritual freedom sacrificed on the day he destroyed the kingfishers' eggs. His guilt peels away and he feels a sense of redemption. Though *Den røde tåken* is anything but a realistic novel, the protagonist's descent resembles what psychologists call the Second Stage of dying, that is, life review and transcendence.[12] The protagonist sees himself bathing in a mountain stream: "He tears off his clothes, dives into the pool, the blue cold water coming from distant mountains. Gets out, shakes off the water. Newborn, more than that, young god, and precisely that: god and young, yes, as though everything no longer existed. A day can be like this, guiltless, a minute can be like this, oh precious minute, it is worth a life."[13] For the first time in the novel the complete episode of Lillegull's murder runs through his mind. The girl's head at last blots out Herman's face. The final pages of *Den røde tåken* are replete with redemption imagery. And redemption clearly is based upon the protagonist's ability to face his own past in a coherent way: "And just now I am in the process of knowing: the past—it returns with its pattern, the inevitable."[14]

It is true that Borgen suggests a Romantic apotheosis—reunification with Lillegull beyond the tomb. However, he stops short and appears to reject such a conclusion emphatically: "And he knows in this falling second, in this fading fragment of half a second, that this is the place towards which he has groped, towards which I now am falling: here, it is here that she lies, lay, shall lie, shall die, in certain eternity, on the spot that the searchers missed, where Lillegull resides, rotten and dead, forever."[15] Far more important than the long chance of union in death with the adolescent who disappeared a generation earlier is the protagonist's ability at last to come to terms with his crime, admit it, denounce the value of the life of action, and see his past whole.

V *The Mythical Allusions*

In the *Lillelord* trilogy, *"Jeg,"* and *Blåtind*, Borgen revealed his fondness for myth. The most important mythic symbol was Nobiskro, a Purgatory derived from German folk belief. To become eligible for liberty and peace the hero must pass through this No-man's Land. Nobiskro also symbolizes the state of mind of the individual who has fallen from innocence and is unable to rid himself of an overwhelming sensation of guilt. The parallel between the quest motifs in Borgen's fiction and the Christian teaching of the fall of man, his exile in the world, his imprisonment in Purgatory, and his ultimate salvation, is fairly obvious. Borgen, however, does not interpret imprisonment and release from Purgatory in any manner resembling the Christian one. For Borgen Purgatory is the consequence of self-inflicted punishment. Liberty from its hold customarily comes in a flash—in *Vi har ham nå* through Wilfred's decision to die, in *"Jeg"* through Matias's decision to tell his story to Sonja, in *Den røde tåken* through the protagonist's discovery of certain verities about existence while at the top of the monolith.

In *Den røde tåken* the monolith has an important allegorical quality. Its chief characteristic is its great height. From the ground it appears to ascend straight to heaven. It is a modern Tower of Babel, the ancient symbol of mankind's desire to measure up to God himself. Several times the protagonist views the structure as a religious object, a divine symbol; and prior to climbing it, the lines of a hymn by the Danish poet N. F. S. Grundtvig flash through his mind.

In the Old Testament the individual who exposed himself

directly to the face of God was condemned to death. The lion of stone atop the monolith, the lion who has no answers for the protagonist, appears to symbolize the deity. As he laboriously gropes his way to the summit of the structure, the protagonist rejects man's natural limitations. His transgression will afford him the opportunity of seeing himself and the human condition from on high. But like an Old Testament prophet who participates in the divine point of view, the protagonist pays for his wisdom with his life. As he descends and his vision expands, he finds the instant invaluable: "Oh precious moment. It is worth a life."

Parallel to the biblical allusions are the classical ones. Multiple references to sight and vision may evoke the Oedipus theme. Abnormally tall, the protagonist bears some physical resemblance to the tragic king of Thebes, whom Sophocles compared to a tower.[16] In daily life the height of the protagonist is a liability. His tub in the hotel is too small for him, his room feels like a cage. But his size becomes a decided asset once he mounts the monolith, since a smaller man could never have accomplished the task. As long as both the protagonist and Oedipus retained their physical vision, spiritual vision was denied them. At the climactic moment of their lives, one loses his spectacles and the other his sight. It is on this occasion that each discovers genuine clarity for the first time in his adult life.

The park containing the monolith evokes the image of the labyrinth hiding the minotaur. Making his way through the park the protagonist refers to the place as a maze that prevents him from reaching his goal: "Strange, no sooner does man get the idea of making something natural, a place for strolling, than he turns it into a kind of labyrinth. Without evil intentions, a man like me attacks a symbol of freedom created to elevate the spirit and god-knows-what. Then I stumble into invisible fences, they force me to make detours and deviations. A kind of spiritual preparation prior to meeting with the divine?"[17] The labyrinth may well symbolize the chaotic state of the protagonist's own mind before his climb.[18] For years a vague, gnawing guilt led him ever more deeply into the maze. It is a commitment to seek his way back to the root of the problem that has provided him with the thread through the labyrinth, leading to his extrication from it and the regaining of his lost liberty.

The protagonist's mind is filled with echoes of literature and myth, much of which, he explains, was absorbed through extensive reading during the five years he spent in prison. He makes direct references to Aristotle and Kierkegaard, quotes hymns and verses from the Bible. He repeatedly compares himself to the city of Jericho, ardently wishing and fearing the collapse of its walls. Once the "walls" surrounding his past are down, he feels certain that he will find liberty and vision. He is equally certain, however, that the price he must pay for liberty is death. He envisions himself as transgressing in order to find liberation— he is a prophet who wishes to see the face of God, or Icarus wishing to transcend human limitations.[19] Before climbing the monolith, as he stands in the window of his hotel room, he foresees what will happen to him: "Total vision: the idea of the tower; distance and freedom. Its punishment: the fall. Not a sparrow shall fall to the ground without its being the sum of all that preceded it, far and near."[20] The protagonist does not doubt for a second that he will have to share the fate of his legendary predecessors who had wanted to participate in divine vision. Unlike Peter Holmgren, he never seriously questions the authority of his beacons, he never considers alternative routes, and he never attempts to compare the "mapped-out course" with the real landscape in front of his eyes. Guided by his faith in myth, he enjoys his moment of vision, and dies from it.

VI *Panoramic Vision and the Work of Art*

As the protagonist falls from the monolith, his experience of dying is virtually an esthetic one. The philosopher Georges Poulet noted how at such a critical moment life review and transcendence can turn the dying person into an artist:

In that certainty of dying, when one is convinced that it is useless to pay further attention to his present life, he falls into a state equivalent to that of the most profound dream: "A human being who would *dream* his existence instead of living it. . . ." This human being, this absolute dreamer, is the dying. Released from all action, freed from the inhibitions that constituted for him his present life, he effortlessly regains possession of his past and of his self.[21]

Therefore Poulet sees the dying person as an artist who totally renounces the world of action for that of introspection. According to Poulet, Proust's Narrator, perched high on the stilts of time at the conclusion of A la Recherche du temps perdu, is similar to a drowning visionary whose past has been transformed into a coherent image.[22] Himself finally able to piece together the fragments of his past, Borgen's falling protagonist enjoys a similar experience. The protagonist's experience can be compared to that of Kierkegaard's Christian, who found salvation when he ventured to throw himself into the depths of the ocean.[23] Far from being of a religious nature, however, the protagonist's instant of joy is that of creative enthusiasm, his grace is esthetic. To use what nearly has become a literary cliché, he is saved through artistic vision, expressed as a meaningful re-creation of his life.

Art plays a significant role in all of Borgen's novels. Wilfred Sagen had been a musician, writer, and painter. But his talents served him poorly; and long before his catharsis in the wilderness he cynically abandoned his work. In Blåtind both Claes and Nathalie possess an artistic bent, and at the novel's end we learn that painting will be crucial to Nathalie's rehabilitation. In Blåtind, however, none of the characters possesses a true artistic vision, and pastiches play a more important role in the novel than original works of art. Peter's profound distrust of words and phrases would in his case render esthetic grace impossible. In "Jeg," on the other hand, matters are different. Matias Roos found that he had to transform reality into words and paragraphs: "He had toyed with writing. It was not his profession, but at times. . . . Had he been required to write it down, he then would have known it all. 'It is my weakness that things have to be written, or at least formed, in order to become real.' "[24] Matias's words are those of an artist. Indeed, he liberates himself from his past only by transforming it into a story.

In Den røde tåken art has an equally significant function. The protagonist lays no claims to being an artist, but his interpretation of reality seems more artistic than that of any other predecessor. Moreover, a work of art is the central symbol in the novel, and it contributes directly to the protagonist's liberation. The carvings on the monolith teach him much about life and the self.

Mythical and literary allusions strengthen the symbolic importance of the monolith. As he mounts the structure, the protagonist genuinely learns to see the world through the artist's eyes. Ultimately he progresses to the point where he makes a total commitment to the esthetic experience. A flash of creative energy rewards him for having rejected life in the world of action for the solitary moment of contemplation. The protagonist imagines the sculptor of the monolith to have been concerned with exploring new ways of conveying old ideas. His originality lay not in what he said but in how he said it.

Taking a backward look through Borgen's fiction, one is astonished by its thematic consistency. Each individual work appears to follow a basic pattern: the hero's "fall" from innocence, his exile in the Nobiskro of the world, his nostalgia for a lost paradise. Customarily a conflicting force, usually female (and in *Lillelord* and *Blåtind* a Jewish female), confronts this antisocial, death-oriented nostalgia by affirming day-to-day reality. From *Lillelord* through *Blåtind* this life-force grows in influence, only to disappear entirely in the pages of *Den røde tåken*. There is no balancing point of view in *Den røde tåken*. Except for a few words exchanged with the reception clerk at the hotel, the protagonist is completely cut off from human contacts. He lives in his own world, communicating merely with the work of art and the ghosts of his past. He seems to possess the solitude that Wilfred so ardently wanted and feared.

While Borgen's male heroes tend to reject realistic, pragmatic solutions to their problems, they nevertheless do not retreat into mystical ones. Having read such stories as "Kaprifolium" and "Natt og dag 1" one might anticipate the latter way out. On the contrary, however, the ocean's mysterious pull, so evident in many of the short stories and present in the *Lillelord* trilogy, disappears from the later novels. Tangible monuments, supposedly containing the answer at their summit, replace the sea as objects of longing. Peter Holmgren fails to reach the peak of "Blåtind." It is too inaccessible for a mere human. But the archetypal climber of *Den røde tåken*, certain of his desire to acquire comprehension of the self and his past, scales the monolith. The summit requires a total commitment on his part, but he never questions his ability to reach it. At the top he opts for suicide.

But he does not see the fall from the top as a defeat. Dropping through space he has sufficient moral strength remaining to expiate a lifetime of guilt and comprehend the wholeness of his past. He has learned how to replace the chaotic torment of diurnal existence with the blissful discovery of awareness through contemplation.

CHAPTER 9

Return to the Other

I Trær alene i skogen

EVERY man is a lead character in his own tiny drama, but in the great game: a secondary character that destiny rejects." Borgen wrote this statement in the epigraph for his most recent collection of short stories, *Trær alene i skogen* (1969). The individual is a single tree in the forest or a soldier in the army. Chop down the tree or kill the soldier; the forest remains and the army still functions. Totally absorbed in their egos, Wilfred Sagen, Matias Roos, Peter Holmgren, and the protagonist in *Den røde tåken* fail to comprehend their insignificance within the framework of human existence. The characters in *Trær alene i skogen* do not wish to conquer the past, climb unattainable mountains, or mount great towers. They are nevertheless lead players in their own humble dramas, and they are defeated by destiny. But they make no pretense of a grand struggle against fate. They lack the Romantic quality of the heroes of Borgen's novels. They are little people.

"Morgen på Montparnasse" ("Morning on Montparnasse") is a very brief story describing a scene observed by the narrator as he looks out the window of his room in Paris's Rue Vavin while waiting for his tea water to boil. He notices a young man, the friend of the girl who lives next door, cross the busy street below with an empty wine container in his hand. Presumably he is going to the bistro on the other side of the street to get his container filled. The young man's girl friend stands in *her* window, and sees him wave to her before he crosses the traffic-laden street. The narrator also notices a group of masons, Italian immigrants, repairing the façade of a building on the other side of the street. They coordinate their movements as gracefully as a troupe of circus acrobats: "From the ground upwards they

129

were handing bricks to one another according to a system so precise that had one hand slipped or one second been wasted, it would have seemed as though the world had perished."[1] The young man going after his wine slips into the Rue Vavin with the grace of a marten, skillfully avoids the cars that are racing all around him, reaches the other side, and once more waves to his girl. Then he enters the bistro for his wine. The workers cease their efforts for a few moments and sit down around the tables on the sidewalk outside the bistro. Then the young man emerges with his container filled, waves once again, and starts to make his way across the street. Suddenly car brakes shriek, drivers jump out of their automobiles and gesticulate, ambulance sirens blare, and the young man lies in the street in a pool of blood and wine. His body is transported into the ambulance, the crowd disintegrates as quickly as it had formed, and the workers return to their job. The narrator sees the girl move toward the spot where her friend had been struck, and she takes the wine container that had been thrown from the accident site. The narrator returns to his tea water.

"Morgen på Montparnasse" tells of the defeat of a small man. Because he, unlike the Italians, permitted his attention to slip or because a driver failed to take heed of his presence, the young man died. His death did not seem to have changed very much. The workers are back with their bricks, other drivers race down the street again, the narrator will eat his breakfast. Perhaps even the girl will resume her activities shortly. The story also tells of instants of small happiness, "the naked NOW without a past, without a future." The movements of the masons at work are all grace and beauty, the wave of the young man to his girl was an endearing caress, sunshine sparkled on the wine container and in the eyes of the Italians. Borgen seems to be saying: seize the small victories in life, savor them. When the defeat is inevitable, these triumphs are what make life tolerable.

"Bipersoner" ("Secondary Characters") is a totally different type of story. The plot concerns incest, murder, and suicide. Mona and Ragnar are a sister and brother who are brought up separately and do not know each other's identity. They are orphans. Both their parents died on the day of Mona's birth. When Ragnar is nineteen and his sister several years younger they happen to meet in Copenhagen. Instinctively sensing Ragnar's identity, Mona seduces him. Ragnar, unaware that Mona is his sister, is seized with disgust and makes an attempt to strangle her. He receives a prison sentence. During his trial the identities of the two are revealed. Two years later, out on parole, Ragnar seeks Mona out and this time does murder her. Again he is caught and arrested. Ragnar becomes the subject of wide publicity in the sensationalist press. His story serves as the point of departure for renewed debates on such diverse issues as the criminal nature of incest, the curse of capitalism, and fluoride in the drinking water. In jail the young man commits suicide. Newspaper editors seem to recall the bizarre case clearly enough to send reporters to Ragnar's funeral in the prison cemetery. Since it is the day to announce the fall fashions, however, the filed stories fail to compete successfully with Balmain's secrets. Out of the tragedy of life the press created and exposed Ragnar and Mona as caricatures to a curious public. To suit the whims of the readers, editors arbitrarily decide whether to revive or inter them. The press used the poor young people to satiate society's fantasies. It had no interest whatsoever in dealing with the pair as human beings, in ferreting out the real reasons that lay behind their tragedy and defeat.

In "Oppstandelse" ("Resurrection") the central character is France's Unknown Soldier. He is the complete victim. A war begun by others killed him; then politicians and generals had his guts scraped up and transported to a box beneath a triumphal arch as a celebration of national pride. The ruling powers betray their cynicism by denying their symbol any sense of individuality. He is the eternal secondary character, a serial number that the leviathan state lost in the shuffle and resurrected to salve its conscience. For Borgen an equally unlikely hero is the protagonist in "Pålitelig og pliktoppfyllende" ("Trustworthy and Dutiful"). This is the night watchman in a factory who for thirty years has been checking the accuracy of the alarm clocks in the place. He has practically no human contacts and does his job diligently. One evening, however, in a fury he smashes every clock in the factory. His superiors attribute this act to an emotional breakdown, but cannot comprehend why he behaved so violently. The answer of course is simple. The watchman simply decided to rebel against a completely revolting, inhuman environment. Before his explosion he had explained to a doctor his feeling on nonidentity: "No, he was no forest pine, no necrology would call him a tree intended for a mast. He was rather a tiny bush, something you walked straight through, for you see, doctor, it is as though no one notices me, I could surely walk straight past the ticket taker on the bus, but do not only because I am an honest man."[2] He makes several attempts to make others notice him, but in vain. The clock-smashing was an anguished cry of revolt and a demand for help. But society apparently still chose not to listen and understand it.

The young man at Montparnasse, Mona and Ragnar, the Unknown Soldier, and the night watchman all are humble individuals who are victimized by the callousness of others. Had the drivers cared about the lives they were endangering, the young man might have made it across the Rue Vavin, had society paid attention to him the night watchman might have secured a grip upon his individuality. The world noticed Ragnar and Mona only when the press sensationalized their misfortune; and authorities defame the senselessness of the Unknown Soldier's death when they parade the glories of national pride before his tomb.

Borgen's latest short stories are particularly interesting because they appear to relinquish the quest motif that dominated his earlier stories as well as the novels from *Lillelord* through *Den røde tåken*. Wilfred Sagen, Matias Roos, Peter Holmgren, and the protagonist of *Den røde tåken* are versions of the Romantic hero indulging in the cult of his ego. To these individuals the rest of the world is composed of "secondary characters." It is quite possible that Borgen himself now regrets having condoned the excessive individualism of most of them. Peter Holmgren is the only one of these characters whose point of view is strongly challenged by another character, and who himself at the end of his life is prepared to change direction.

A curious dialogue takes place in *Trær alene i skogen*. It is called "Robert 60." In it a nearly forgotten character from the *Lillelord* trilogy, Wilfred's friend Robert, confronts the author with a complaint. Robert accuses Borgen of having treated him with untoward arrogance, as a character unworthy of real attention. He is given neither a surname nor a physical description. He inherits what Wilfred, in his all-consuming quest for innocence, isolation, and death, discards—including a mistress. Robert believes that the author considered him to be an uninteresting character simply because he had come to terms with life. Like Wilfred, he had carried a burden of personal guilt. As a boy in a sailing regatta, he had wished to win a race so badly that he failed to rescue an individual who had fallen into the water and subsequently drowned. During the First World War Robert became a leading profiteer. Like Wilfred, Robert had known the temptation of Romantic individualism. Had he not at all times carried Hamsun's *Pan* in his pocket? But during the Second World War, Robert learned to rid himself of much of his guilt, and especially of impossible resolutions of it. He came to accept his personality for what it was and achieve even a small amount of this-world heroism by participating in the Resistance. Wilfred of course interpreted Robert's activity with characteristic cynicism, and Borgen prejudiced the reader against him by stressing, among other things, Robert's interest in cornering the manufacture of posters—especially political ones —once the occupation drew to a close. In "Robert 60" the character is allowed to defend his choice before an author who is possibly tired of having glorified the complex superhero at the expense of the ordinary man. Most people, says Robert, seek out psychological harmony in their compromises with life. He adds that this is not a very literary solution. It is a banal one, but nevertheless "fairly and squarely what is true."[3] Back in *Vi har ham nå*, Robert defended his position to Wilfred in similar terms.[4] However, at that point, the hero rejected it unequivocally, and the author's stand was at best ambiguous.

In his subsequent novels, excluding *Blåtind* perhaps, the Romantic solution to his heroes' identity crises remained the major option for Borgen. In *Trær alene i skogen* the secondary characters fail to remain passive any longer, and attempt in a small way to revolt against the forces that had denied them genuine identity. The night watchman smashes the clocks, the ghost of the Unknown Soldier leaves the grave and frightens to death a general making a speech by the flame, Robert takes his revenge on the author. In Borgen's latest novel, *Min arm, min tarm* (*My Arm, My Intestine*), the reexamination becomes complete and Robert's successor indeed prevails.

II Min arm, min tarm

Structurally and stylistically, *Min arm, min tarm* has little in common with the allegorical representations in "*Jeg*" and *Den røde tåken.* Neither does Borgen return to the detailed descriptions of the *Lillelord* trilogy. In his latest novel fantasy and even black humor surface; medical reports, police reports, newspaper articles, letters, and the thoughts of the protagonist mingle with conventional conversation to contribute to a casual, rapid-flowing style. It is the only one of Borgen's novels which is distinctly comic. The events in the novel take place in the recent past, the present, and the near future, terminating in October, 1973, that is, a year following the actual publication date of the novel. Borgen refers to episodes and incidents that captured the interest of the Norwegian public in 1972, ranging from the great national debate over the Common Market to a series of sensational post office robberies near Oslo. Unlike Borgen's previous novels which were turned toward the past, *Min arm, min tarm* concerns itself with the realities of today and tomorrow. The protagonist is a young man who learns to appreciate the attractions of the future.

III *The Plot*

On March 22, 1972, a thirty-two-year-old college French teacher, Frank G. Vegårdshei, has an operation for a duodenal ulcer. The novel opens as Frank is regaining consciousness, and the action takes place during his period of recovery. During Frank's stay at the hospital he becomes involved in a serious matter. One of his roommates, Tom Olsen, who is suffering from a severe liver ailment, asks Frank to get him a bottle of port. Frank obtains permission to leave the hospital for a short time, buys the wine, and smuggles it in to Tom. Tom drinks the contents of the bottle, suffers an attack, and dies. Shortly thereafter Frank is transferred to a convalescent home and fails in a suicide attempt. Then he flees the home, visits a semiretired psychiatrist, and decides to run away from Norway. He goes to

Paris, where he had lived as a student ten years before. His complicity in Tom's death continues to plague him. So does his role in a fatal automobile accident that had occurred more than a year before. In January, 1971, Frank's car had collided with a vehicle driven by a Swede. The Swede died of injuries sustained in the accident. The police report exonerated Frank, who married Kamma, the victim's widow, four months after the crash. The marriage lasted less than a year, and Frank is obsessed with hatred of his estranged wife. He believes her to be a witch, who is casting a spell over him.

While in Paris, Frank visits the Jardin des Plantes and is fascinated by the caged apes there. A gorilla whom he privately calls Horox interests him particularly, and one day Frank manages to worm his way into the beast's cage. The ape seizes Frank and probably would have killed him had a policeman and a guard not come to his rescue. Some cameramen telecasting a program nearby in the Jardin spot Frank in the gorilla's cage, and immediately focus their equipment upon him. Frank thereby becomes somewhat of a public figure. He refuses to give the police his identity, however. In Frank's pockets the police find cards bearing the name and address of a certain Gerard Molineux. Frank nods agreement when the officers ask if he is Molineux, and the police accompany him to the address indicated on the cards. Molineux, it turns out, is a sixty-year-old sculptor whom Frank had recently met in a bar. When the police ring his bell, Molineux accepts the strange situation without asking any questions. But the publicity surrounding Frank's escapade is so great that as a result of public pressure, the police return the following day and arrest him. Jailed for a couple of days, Frank is rescued by his estranged wife, Kamma. She obtains his release and also informs him that she is pregnant by another man. He returns to Oslo. Nearly a year passes. The final two chapters of the novel take place in the early fall of 1973. Frank has bought a small farm, where he settles with Kamma's baby, a mulatto child called Jeanette. Kamma now has divorced him, and, as a journalist, leaves the country to tour Hanoi and other trouble spots around the world.

The plot in *Min arm, min tarm* is fantastic and often outrageous. But it is no more fantastic than the chaos raging in

Frank's mind. He is a physically and mentally ill person who is trying to recover. Before he succeeds he must rid himself of the guilt he feels for having been an accessory to two deaths, and he must come to terms with his suicidal tendencies. He must overcome the mental confusion that plagues him at the novel's commencement. Appropriately enough, the novel opens with a semiconscious Frank perceiving the distant voice of a nurse who says: "Frank! You must wake up now!" *Min arm, min tarm* is an account of Frank's awakening; it tells of his odyssey from the world of fantasy into human reality. More important, it also is the statement of a novelist who wishes at seventy to modify his esthetic philosophy.

IV *Frank's Illness*

Like *Den røde tåken, Min arm, min tarm* is told in a third-person narrative with an omniscient author and Frank's interlocutors focusing almost exclusively upon the protagonist's problems. Frank reports several of his thought sequences in the third person as well, as though to underscore his identity crisis. This is a technique which Borgen explored with considerable success in *"Jeg"* and *Den røde tåken*. At the beginning of *Min arm, min tarm* Frank shows classic schizoid tendencies, and his ulcer seems to have been related to his mental stress. Frank has lost touch with reality. During his adult life he seems to have had little contact with the outside world. His work as a teacher of college French has brought him little gratification through communication with others. In fact, one of his major problems was precisely his inability to communicate. As he thinks back upon it from his hospital bed, his professional life seems unreal: "Doesn't remember, remembers less and less from that world, it seems distant. Or unreal, perhaps rather that, unthinkable to return, the whole thing is an illusion."[5] Frank's only professional acquaintance was a colleague called Fred Brink. The basis for their friendship was the fact that students would pun their similar first names. During this time phonetics had great importance for Frank. Sublimating his lack of human contacts, he used to create entire verbal systems. But human contacts were another matter. He was a virtual exile from the society in which he nevertheless existed.

Frank has no idea of his place in the world. In his hospital ward he meditates upon the relationship of his operation to his existence. He sees his body as a combination of interchangeable parts over which he has no control. Frank lacks a will. Situations engulf him. When a man half-dead from a liver ailment shoves a bill into his hand and requests a bottle of port wine, Frank blindly submits to the wishes of the other. He lacks the sense of responsibility and involvement necessary to conceive of the consequence. When a nurse asks whether he will accompany her to his doctor, who wishes to see him, he thinks half in scorn, half in resignation: "Of course he is coming. The dog always comes when the master calls...."[6] Frank sees himself as an object that others manipulate according to their whims. He has no independent personality, but is composed of layers that respond mechanically to the roles others request of him. In keeping with other Borgen characters, the source of Frank's troubles lies in the past, in his childhood and youth.

V *The Past*

Frank's past is shorter than that of Borgen's other protagonists. Matias Roos and the main character in *Den røde tåken* were in their late middle age. At the conclusion of the *Lillelord* trilogy Wilfred Sagen was forty-five, and his exhaustion had made him seem older. Peter and Nathalie in *Blåtind* were in their midthirties. By contrast, Frank Vegårdshei is in his early thirties. His childhood is only twenty years past, his student days in Paris a fresh memory. Prior to coming to the hospital one of the major crises in his life, his automobile accident, is only a little over a year in the past.

Frank's memories of childhood are dominated by the ambitions adults had for him and his consequential fears of being a loser.[7] His mother had died when he was very young, and his Aunt Klara helped to rear him. She would warn him that the world does not tolerate losers. He recalls her voice singing the round of a children's game in which the loser ended up in a great black cauldron. Frank always used to see himself as headed for the cauldron. His father was ambitious for him, and he felt

that he would never live up to the elder Vegårdshei's expecta-
tions. Frank's fears increased in adolescence. Moreover, the
loser's image was by now so ingrained in him that he felt
unable to accept any sign of reward. He was sent to the *lycée*
for Norwegians in Rouen at his father's and aunt's expense. At
the moment he was to receive his diploma he was paralyzed with
fright. He was unable even to walk to the front of the hall and
accept the document. Again, as a student at the Sorbonne, he
collapsed from fear rather than give a talk which he had prepared meticulously.

Frank nevertheless completed his studies successfully and
anticipated the moment when he could lay his Sorbonne diploma
in his father's hand. But upon his return to Oslo, his hope was
shattered. He found his father dying, unable to comprehend
that his son was a winner at last: "And so, at the decisive
moment when he returned with his palms and bananas, ready to
regain the paternal confidence—the secret dream of all depraved
sons—he [the father] is concentrating entirely upon a situation
[dying] which of course may be important enough for the person concerned. And thereupon the gaunt palms of the chapel
take over."[8]

Frank took a teaching job because that is what an individual
with a Sorbonne degree in French is supposed to do. The post
bored him, but he courageously developed his word games in
an attempt to convince himself that his work was important.
Human contacts eluded him. After several uneventful years the
moment struck that changed his life. He had been driving along
a two-lane highway at nearly ninety miles per hour. A Swedish
vehicle coming in the other direction suddenly veered and
crashed into his automobile. The driver of the other car, a certain
Mr. Jolin, was killed instantly. His wife, who was a passenger,
suffered a broken arm. Frank miraculously escaped with a light
brain concussion. The police investigation found Mr. Jolin at
fault. It was assumed that, as a Swede, he had been confused
by Norway's right-hand traffic. Kamma Jolin corroborated this.
Neither she nor Frank admitted that the Norwegian had been
speeding. Four months after the accident Kamma and Frank
were married. The marriage quickly proved unworkable, the
couple agreed to a trial separation, and Frank believed himself

to be in the cauldron again. He would refer to the late Mr. Jolin as "the Swedish pig" and in his mind Kamma was incarnated as a witch. Hers is the evil eye that had recognized Frank's guilt even though she did not admit it to the authorities. Why had Frank married Kamma in the first place? The reasons are not clear. Masochism? A sealed victory over Mr. Jolin? Love? As Frank's wife, Kamma took the place of Aunt Klara and his father. She was the dominating force in their brief life together. Frank resented this. He acquired his ulcer over it and found a new shelter of protection in the hospital.

VI *The Quest for Nothingness*

In the hospital Frank luxuriates in the fact that he is just an object, an intestine that requires maximum care to begin functioning normally again. Whenever memories appear, provoking fear and guilt, a merciful nurse just pushes a needle into his arm and he descends into solitude and nothingness: "Wonder-ful—Wonderful day that turns into night, that turns into morning. No fear. Nothing, not even himself, wonderful nothingness."[9] Frank imagines himself sliding down a singing stream, dissolving into it. But, unlike the little boy in the honeysuckle vine ("Kapritolium") he has no experience of becoming All. On the contrary, he becomes Nobody. He neither seeks nor finds identity with the universe, but merely a convenient escape from the problems of the present. Moreover, Frank's adventures are little more than games, since he knows that the pills do not place him in danger of losing consciousness permanently. On the contrary, he will shortly awaken in his comfortable hospital bed. There is nothing positive in Frank's need for dissolution of his personality. Even later, when he attempts suicide, we are led to doubt the sincerity of Frank's action.

It is the death of Tom Olsen that causes Frank to seek out the ultimate nothingness; but his half-hearted attempt at suicide is a failure. Meanwhile his intestine heals amidst his insistence that it is just a part of his anatomy unrelated to all the rest. He runs away from the convalescent home where he tried to kill himself, and he finds a semiretired psychiatrist. He confides to the psychiatrist his complicity in the deaths of Tom and Mr.

Jolin. When he mentions the victims he becomes violent. His hands reach out for an imaginary throat, his body becomes convulsive, he grunts. The psychiatrist explains that Frank now possesses the self-image of a murderer, not a loser. Frank believes that a suppressed primitive side of himself was responsible for the deaths of the two men. It was his authentic personality, and it is surfacing. Frank promises to feed his primitive side, and the psychiatrist fears that other lives, particularly Kamma's, are in danger. But he makes no attempt to restrain Frank, who leaves his office, and decides to go to Paris.

VII *The Failure of Primitivism*

In Frank's mind Paris signifies liberation. Borgen does not say precisely why, but it probably has to do with the years Frank spent there as a student. Kamma appears to have lived in Paris as well, and Frank does look for her in an apartment building where she had once stayed. He does not find her. Above all, however, in Paris Frank believes he can give free play to his newly discovered primitive side. The city reeks with animals—dead, alive, and in stone. Frank lives and eats excessively. He recalls with pleasure the popular myth that the French indiscriminately consume all types of birds and animals—sparrow, starling, cat, dog. He loves to visit the zoo in the Jardin des Plantes. He experiences a desire to climb the lion monument at the Place Denfert-Rochereau. The traffic on the Place de la Concorde makes him think of a vipers' nest. Frank is fascinated by the absurd belief of a French bar acquaintance, Gerard Molineux. Molineux informs Frank that worms which devour other worms acquire the characteristics of their victims. Frank thinks that the same may be true with humans. He feels that he has absorbed Tom Olsen. Tom's need to drink the port wine was a bestial desire: "He wanted to have his debauch and die from it."[10] Frank reads the rebellious verses of Villon and dreams of murdering Kamma. He scorns human traits and begins to idolize a huge gorilla in the Jardin des Plantes. He names the beast Horox, which in his private language means "the horrible one."

One day before Horox's cage Frank launches into a diatribe

against the human species, the only one that kills for the sake of killing. Misplaced pride has caused man to set himself above all other creatures on the great chain of being, but in reality man should be at the bottom. He is "flatter than the worm." Frank's monologue frightens him, and he sinks to his knees in hopes of being liberated from his degrading portrait of humanity. When nothing happens, he decides that Horox must be awarded the place in the hierarchy which man has usurped from him. He will change places with the gorilla. Somehow Frank finds a way to enter Horox's cage on his hands and knees. As he does so, he finds new pleasure in primitivism. He becomes "a creature returning home to an unknown animal realm."[11] Horox immediately jolts him out of his reverie, however, by lifting him bodily and pummeling him against the bars of the cage. A guard and a policeman rescue Frank. Later, in an explanation of his conduct to the police, Horox states: "I was so irritated by this intellectual's unceasing degradation of mankind as such . . . that—in spite of the fact that violence is against my gorilla nature—I was tempted to use purely human means against him."[12] Later Frank learns—from Kamma—that his confrontation with Horox had appeared on French television. "All of Paris was laughing," she adds.[13]

The laughter of the Parisians underscores the absurdity of Frank Vegårdshei's quest, a parody of a quest really. The surname Borgen has chosen for his protagonist emphasizes the farcical element. "Vegårdshei" seems to parody a Norwegian country name.[14] Frank Vegårdshei's adventure in Paris is the provincial Norwegian intellectual's absurd attempt to find his authentic, primitive self in a zoo in the cultural capital of Europe. Frank's quest for primitivism was merely another attempt to rid himself of responsibility for the deaths of Tom Olsen and Mr. Jolin.[15] It also permitted him to rationalize his hatred of Kamma. He even persuaded himself that the "authentic" thing to do would be to kill her. When the police request Frank's identity, he remains mute. This makes sense, for at this point he has no idea who he is. His latest effort to find identity had just ended in miserable failure. When asked whether he is Gerard Molineux, the individual whose cards have been found in his pockets, Frank nods affirmatively. He has returned to his old habit of allowing himself to be carried along by situations rather than attempting to control them. On this occasion, however, fate is with Frank. The Frenchman turns out to be the correct person to show Frank where he has gone astray and how he will regain balance in his life.

VIII *The Problem of the Other*

Until the moment he enters Molineux's apartment Frank finds it impossible to establish any sort of meaningful relationship with others. In his quest for identity he needs other people only as they serve his own ends. While nourishing a dream of "companionship," Frank in reality is completely egocentric. In the hospital he became embittered when a roommate, old Aslaksen, was dying, for the man occupied all the attention of the nurses. On his return from Paris, diploma in hand, Frank resented the fact that his own dying father had been unable to appreciate the son's academic success. For Frank other people exist only to confirm his own existence. He has no interest in them as individuals, with personalities and problems of their own.[16]

Frank must avoid all human involvement. He sees this as a sign of maturity: "One day a person has to become adult enough not to give a damn about other people."[17] He is equally determined not to permit others to probe his feelings. When he runs away from the sanitarium, he goes directly to a psychiatrist; when questioned by him, however, Frank sees him as an antagonist. Except for the nurses coming to drug him, Frank rejects all offers of help. When he went to get Tom Olsen's port wine, he nearly fainted in the street. An elderly lady offered assistance. He rebuffed her: "Thank you very much. I say thank you very much madam . . . but I get along perfectly."[18] Nothing, of course, is further from the truth. The ways out he selects are all dead ends.

Frank's reactions toward others are based upon fear. His father and aunt instilled within him a morbid fear of failure. On the other hand, Frank dreaded competition. He even viewed his kindly uncle in London, Sebastian, "an institution of solidity, of safety," as safety "with a built-in threat."[19] Later on, as an adult, Frank experienced meetings with others as collisions, during which he exposed himself to the risk of physical and mental damage. His automobile accident was a particularly concrete and violent illustration of what occurs on a psychic level whenever two people meet. His marriage to Kamma was a steady stream of mental collisions, similar to what Strindberg called "the battle of the brains." After their separation, Frank thinks of her as his old adversary: "Kamma: something with teeth, showing its teeth, something voracious, something that *wants,* that wants something special all the time. Something against which one has to defend himself, always, something against which one must continue to defend himself, always, something against which one must become Horox. Always. Remember it, Frank, remember it. Defend himself, must always defend himself."[20] Kamma, Frank believes, will devour him, annihilate him, unless he is able first to annihilate her.

In the light of Frank's defensiveness regarding others, Kamma proves to be a disaster for him. She is a liberated, intelligent woman, sensitive to the needs of others. She is self-confident and efficient. Her love for Frank was based upon a desire to help him, and she has a knack for getting him out of embarrassing situations, including his responsibility for the death of Mr. Jolin and his brief imprisonment in Paris. When Frank runs away from the sanitarium, good newspaper reporter that she is, Kamma follows his tracks to the psychiatrist, Paris, and Molineux's apartment. When she at last catches up with him in jail, she arranges his release. Her efficiency, however, reminds Frank of his own incompetence. He is unable to hide a thing from her. She strips him naked. Therefore he turns her into a witch, the "evil eye." Frank's egoism, fear of human contacts, and realization of Kamma's superiority made the marriage unendurable for him. Kamma gave him his ulcer and unknowingly set him along the road of his quest.

Frank's journey ends in the apartment of Gerard Molineux. When the police deposit Frank there, Molineux takes him in without question. He gives him something to eat and drink, dresses his wounds, and encourages him to get a good night's sleep. On the following day Molineux has a long conversation with Frank and offers him some sage advice. He informs Frank that the Norwegian's situation is not particularly astonishing or unique: "Most of what happens is trifling, we humans have the weakness of making too much out of everything, it is not good for our mental balance...."[21] According to Molineux, Frank is the victim of an uncontrollable imagination, that converts trifles into overblown events. Because he always has done this, Frank has missed discovering his own insignificance. He has constructed his life upon myths—first the myth of defeatism, then the myth of mysticism, then the myth of primitivism. Finally, he has made a myth of Kamma, an unfair one: "I don't believe in witches," Molineux says. "I don't believe in the evil eye. But I believe in bewitched individuals...."[22]

Molineux finds Frank bewitched by his own fixations. The Frenchman relates a little allegory built upon his own experience as a circus performer. High-wire acrobats, he says, are extremely superstitious. They are always interpreting signs and pronouncing ritual formulas. Once they perform their act, however, they rid themselves of dependence upon magic. They rely only upon their skill, powers of concentration, and confidence in their partners. Should they give themselves over to their myths while on the wire, they are doomed. Molineux insists that self-control, self-discipline, and concentration are the essence of life:

The vast majority of these brave people humiliate themselves vis-à-vis a primitive outgrowth of some presumed divinity, they call themselves religious and probably are in a way, not unlike sailors in need at sea. But in the working moment—when the artist is whirling around up there and is to the millimeter dependent upon his concentration, and that of his partner, when they are floating around, pierced by the limelights, then they are at the same time leaving behind all their vague notions of protective deities. All accidents, catastrophes, are caused by the human factor, and that means simply that concentration slips during a split second or so. Then it would be fatal to think about God.[23]

"God," to Molineux, means any myth or fascination that would intervene with man's ability to think in a clear, rational way. Later Kamma informs Frank that Molineux's wisdom is not at all theoretical, but rather based upon wide and practical experience of life. His own wife, herself a circus acrobat, had perished in a fall. Molineux has no use for vapid intellectualizing, or pseudo-mystic quests. He would reject out of hand the searches of all previous Borgen heroes—Wilfred Sagen's hunt for innocence and peace that concluded in his death, Matias Roos's quest for an undefinable frontier that resulted in withdrawal from society, Peter Holmgren's futile struggle to attain "Blåtind," Claes Hermelin's fascination with Peter's corpse, the climb and fall of the protagonist in *Den røde tåken.* Upon arriving in Molineux's apartment, Frank too was about to plunge. But, as he discovers, "Molineux had caught him in the fall."[24]

It seems safe to presume that, while there are important differences between the Frenchman and Borgen, the former nevertheless serves as a *porte-parole* for the novelist. Throughout Borgen's work we have seen how fantasy, myth, and dream pulled the protagonists away from practical reality, toward isolation, art, or death. Art was the one positive result of the fascination with the quest for identity. This is a notion Borgen, through Molineux, now seems to have modified. Creative fantasy, the sculptor says, "is an extension of experience."[25] The function of the artist is to make his life experience available to others, and by so doing, hopefully help others achieve in their own lives a degree of mental balance. Far from marking a sudden shift in Borgen's thought, this view would be a natural result of the duality we have seen in virtually all of his previous works. Borgen's heroes have great appetites: they devour experiences, books, even other people's personalities. But what do they learn? This is a central problem in *Min arm, min tarm.* The experience conveyed in the novel is that the intellectualized quest for identity is a cover-up for an inability to deal with the problems of life. Thanks to Molineux, Frank realizes this, learns his lesson, and is able to reorient his existence.

For Frank, Molineux serves as a father—the father perhaps that Wilfred never found. Molineux is an artist of utmost sincerity. He describes himself as a sculptor without ambitions. His pieces are not tortured representations of a chaotic soul, but realistic representations of animals and birds, made of plaster and wood. It is interesting to notice, however, that Molineux does not address Frank through his art. He opts for the more direct approach of the simple, paternal sage. When he had first arrived in Paris, hoping to revel in his primitivism, Frank was devoted to François Villon's "testaments" to unadorned individualism. When he returns to Oslo, having indeed learned from his experience and Molineux's wisdom, Frank has both feet on the ground at last. He has abandoned Villon, and the Romantic approach toward life no longer appeals.

In his final encounters with Frank, the reader has the sentiment that the character simply has accepted life on its own terms. He has bought a farm and settles on it with Kamma's child, Jeanette. The last chapter of the novel takes place in the near future, in October, 1973: "Silent fall all around. Open. The October storm removed the last foliage. Like a complete housecleaning, Frank thinks."[26] The protagonist has escaped from the circles in which Borgen's previous heroes were entrapped and is able to direct his energies toward an open-ended future. The ghosts of the past are nearly gone. He no longer hates Kamma. It was he who proposed to take her child—the first time in his relationship with her that he was the active agent. What he proposes to Kamma is nothing less than a rejection of the traditional male-female roles in favor of roles deliberately chosen by the individual himself. No longer the egoist, Frank drops his quest for identity and permits his thoughts to center on Jeanette. He is consciously struggling to rid himself of his fascination with word games. He becomes father and mother of the little mulatto child. Frank's reactions toward others change. A busy cashier in the supermarket becomes a "terrific person" simply because she takes the time to smile to Jeanette. Frank's newly gained serenity is tested when the police mistakenly identify him as a suspect in a post office robbery. As he sits in the kitchen awaiting the arrival of the interrogators, Frank displays a calm that contrasts markedly with Wilfred Sagen's longing for flight in the final pages of *Vi har ham nå*. When he hears the Resistance worker in the stairwell, Wilfred almost automatically pulls the trigger. This is his ultimate refusal to confront his pursuers. Frank, on the other hand, has lost his fear of others. When the knock strikes his door, he opens it and says straightforwardly: "I am Frank Vegårdshei." He says to himself: "I am no longer Nobody, I am Frank."[27] The significance of the name is self-evident.

Curiously enough, Frank discovers his identity only after he has ceased his self-centered quest for it. Like Robert in the trilogy, he learns simply to accept the past and the present. To achieve this, Robert had to give up Hamsun, Frank had to abandon Villon. Instead of an impossible quest for childhood, he directs his energies toward carving out a future for a real child that needs him. He anticipates the future, a future with Jeanette whom he hopes to save from the "cauldron" he once knew. Ironically, he is the only one of Borgen's protagonists who finds both a sense of identity and of childlike innocence. Frank has rejected the quest as a self-deceiving, dangerous fantasy that turns the individual into a perpetual fugitive. For the first time in his life he wishes to give of himself to another.[28] Above all, Frank sheds the skin of a would-be Romantic hero. Just as he can live without his intestine, he learns that the world can exist without him. But just as the parts of his body relate to his entire organism—both mental and physical—so does Frank relate to humanity. While Kamma goes into the world to expose corruption and assist others through her writings, Frank will remain home and tend to her baby. Both will do their part. Frank knows that his troubles are far from over. The police still suspect that he has been implicated in the post office robbery, Kamma may return and claim Jeanette. A cold winter will follow the cleansing autumn. Nevertheless, he remains confident about the future. "We'll make it," he would say to the little girl by his side.

CHAPTER 10

Conclusion

IN his address on H. C. Branner at the University of Oslo, Borgen said: "Whatever Branner's topic happens to be and whatever types of people he writes about, the conflict always deals with essential matters—with good forces and bad forces."[1] While in Borgen's own work it is impossible to qualify the forces tugging at the protagonist as being "good" or "bad," the fact remains that, as with Branner, the concern is for essentials. Alienation, guilt, nostalgia for innocence—these are the coherent themes that run through the Borgen corpus. Yet in each of his works Borgen poses the problem in a different light, and the change of focus in turn modifies the solution.

The starting point for Borgen rests with his fundamental discontent over the quality of existence in the contemporary world. The protagonists in his novels are all bourgeois intellectuals painfully aware of the Nobiskro of their soul. Unlike the majority who live out their shadow lives alternating between boredom and worldly ambition, these characters sense existence to be a puppetlike routine. Eliot best sums up their plight in his "Third Quartet":

> Neither plenitude nor vacancy. Only a flicker
> Over the strained, time-ridden faces
> Distracted from distraction by distraction
> Filled with fancies and empty of meaning
> Tumid apathy with no concentration.[2]

But how to escape? Borgen's heroes are unable to use as guides the moral and religious myths that led previous generations out of their spiritual wastelands. As modern men profoundly aware of their liberty, they construct their own aids. In Borgen's short stories many protagonists appear to opt for mysticism—built upon a collapse of the will and longing for dissolution, even death.

148

In several short stories, the *Lillelord* trilogy, *"Jeg," Blåtind*, and *Den røde tåken*, the protagonists seek release from Nobiskro by trying to re-create the authenticity of their childhood—which, however, constantly eludes them. Borgen's heroes associate their need to escape with a longing for some unattainable object: Wilfred Sagen buries himself in caves in order to find the foetal egg, Matias hearkens after an ever-receding frontier, Peter Holmgren continues to move toward "Blåtind" while mocking his own belief that purity resides on a mountaintop, Frank Vegårdshei considers his salvation to lie beneath a gorilla's skin. Borgen emphasizes his heroes' anticipation of reward rather than conquest of their goals. His characters resemble the protagonist of Kafka's *The Castle*. Their quests for authenticity remind one of Beckett's Molloy in search of the womb.

Free to select their guides, Borgen's characters nevertheless are imprisoned in their diurnal existence. Curiously enough, their quests often lead them to new versions of confinement— Wilfred and Peter Holmgren in their caves, Matias Roos and Peter in self-constructed circles, Frank Vegårdshei in a gorilla's cage. Once more this brings to mind Beckett's characters. Molloy finds himself trapped in ditches, "the Unnamable" continues his quest within the confines of a container. The enclosures that persistently imprison Borgen's protagonists suggest of course that the genuine source of their difficulties is not bourgeois society as much as their own mental conditions. In *Malone Dies*, Beckett's narrator experiences his room as a prison containing six walls of solid bone.[3] Likewise, Borgen's characters are imprisoned inside their own skulls.

These characters lean heavily upon art and works of art in their attempts to escape from Nobiskro. This is reasonable, since Borgen often seems to envision art as a quasi-religion, provoking a crisis of consciousness that draws the sensitive individual out of the superficial glory of the world and into a deeper level of existence. As young men Wilfred and even Robert devour the early novels of Knut Hamsun, whom Wilfred refers to as the Great One, the Poet, or Father. Both carry copies of *Pan* in their pockets in a way that resembles the manner in which religious Norwegians might carry the New Testament. While Matias Roos never mentions Kafka specifically, his vision of reality closely

resembles that of Joseph K., as is shown by the search for a
frontier, the example of the guards who refuse to accept Matias's
identity papers, and the very tendency toward a metamorphosed
reality. The influence of Hamsun is more subtle. *Pan* is no longer
a book in the protagonist's pocket, but a character in Matias's
own fiction. Similarly, in *Den røde tåken* it is a work of plastic
art, the great monolith, that offers the climber a mythic message
he believes to be of supreme importance in his quest. Finally,
in *Min arm, min tarm* the late-medieval French poet François
Villon guides Frank Vegårdshei away from reality and into the
au-delà. Only half jokingly, Frank refers to the volume of Villon's
poetry in his pocket as his hymn book.

On this last occasion, however, Borgen stops short and questions the salutary influence of the artist as guide. Villon stands for
basically the same things as the early Hamsun—the artist as the
misunderstood outsider, with eternal loneliness as his destiny;
art as superior to life and contemplation as superior to action;
freedom as preferable to involvement and dream to reality. The
poet tells Frank to *withdraw* from the problems of life that plague
him, and Frank must admit that he bears his Villon, not as the
seeker carries his Holy Scripture, but as "the potential suicide
carries his vial of poison." In Hamsun's early novel *Mysteries* the
hero Nagel, an unsuccessful artist, always bears *his* vial with
him and ends up walking into the sea. The dogma of the artist
may indeed produce masterpieces, but it also may destroy the
individual who fails to transpose his existence in such a manner.
It killed Nagel, and in Borgen's work it helps destroy Wilfred
Sagen, Peter Holmgren, and the anonymous climber in *Den
røde tåken*. Matias Roos survived because he succeeded in transforming his anguish into a story. Robert and Frank Vegårdshei
survive and prevail only because they see the danger in time and
cast the vial of poison away. Indeed, artistic beacons do guide
Borgen's protagonists through the wasteland. At the far end,
however, there is either creativity or death. Throughout his work
Borgen has kept pointing this out. In his discussion of *Mysteries*,
published in *Vinduet* in 1959, he wrote: "Already the [novel's]
first 10 pages tell us very clearly that *Mysteries* is a novel about
an artist. And more precisely: about an artist in the moment of
conception, or the moment of destruction. The two are one and

the same when confronted with the *task*.... The moment of conception lasts all through the novel—300 pages. There was to be no birth for Nagel. He was destroyed."[4] Borgen's own novels as well deal with artists in the moment of conception. Only Matias gives birth to a work of art: like Nagel, most of the others are destroyed. By the time he reaches his latest novel, Borgen appears to be asking whether there may be some alternative to the harsh choice offered up by the guides of art. Indeed, a sense of sharing, a return to the world, though not, however, as society's puppet, would be a more appropriate way of taking leave of Nobiskro and attaining psychological peace.

In Borgen's work death is closely associated with the quest motif. Frank Vegårdshei chooses a cemetery in which to contemplate Villon. Borgen's protagonists wander into water, enclose themselves in tomblike caves, and circle aimlessly in ice and snow. They place their lives in danger, and those who love them—and who also ardently desire to free them from Nobiskro—valiantly struggle to place them onto another path. In his short stories Borgen presented a choice between the warmth of human affection and the icy cold of the solitary quest.[5] Most often the hero failed to heed the pleas of the beloved or heard the call after it was too late. In the novels Wilfred Sagen exemplifies the individual who may select either route. Unable to comprehend Hamsun's message he is trapped in Mrs. Frisaksen's outstretched net. Most of his life he prefers the recluse's beacon to that of Miriam. Only after reaching a point where he no longer can change direction does Wilfred suddenly realize that he may have opted for a wrong turning. The same holds true for Peter Holmgren, who literally freezes to death dreaming of warmth, summer, and other human beings. When he chooses to lie down beside Peter's corpse rather than accompany Nathalie away from "Blåtind," Claes Hermelin seems inclined to follow his cousin's example. The very names Miriam and Nathalie symbolize birth; but the men whom they love seem irresistibly drawn toward death.

Thus Borgen's heroes are torn between two types of guides who offer to lead them out of Nobiskro, and it is difficult for the protagonists to distinguish between the "good" and "bad" forces. Borgen himself certainly hesitates in making a qualitative

distinction, at least until *Min arm, min tarm*. The temptations of
art and solitude are considerable, even though they may destroy
the seeker. Nevertheless, there are important instances preceding
Min arm, min tarm where life and love appear preferable. For
example, Borgen seems to mock Peter's choice—Peter mocks it
himself—and the novelist's sympathies lean toward Nathalie. On
the other hand, *Den røde tåken*, the novel which followed
Blåtind, is the most introspective of them all. The protagonist
had made his choice, a commitment to conquer a work of art
and die, even before the novel opens. And unlike any other seeker
in the Borgen corpus, he actually reaches his intended goal.
Still, even the climber in *Den røde tåken* is at times critical of the
artist-guide. Early in the novel he thinks of Kierkegaard's philosophy as luxurious nonsense, and is toying with the idea of
liberating himself from the influence of the Dane.[6] As he scales
the monolith and beholds its carvings he scornfully imagines the
bourgeois existence of the artist who created the monument.[7] He
takes pleasure in urinating on the carved figures.[8] But he never
really questions his own commitment to climb to the summit.
When he reaches the lion, he even rejoices in a sense of poetic
serenity. But the work of art, in itself, holds no positive message
to live by. The lion is cold and silent. Having concluded his
quest and learned this message, the climber carries out his
decision to die, and as he falls, comes to terms with the guilt
that has plagued him all his life.

Completely alone, devoid of human contacts, engaged in a
self-dialogue, the climber in *Den røde tåken* is Borgen's archetypal seeker. His quest is successful, but fatal. He has fewer
doubts about his undertaking than other Borgen seekers, and
he feels amply rewarded by his vision during the fall. His quest
contrasts with that of Peter, who considered himself a clown
and a joker, of Wilfred, whose grimaces were those of a comedian,
and finally of Frank Vegårdshei, whose quest is so absurd that
it appears to parody those of his predecessors. Initially, Frank
needs medical drugs and sleeping pills to pull himself out of
Nobiskro; and the mystic state their use produces is itself a
caricature.[9] Frank's choice of primitivism as a way of achieving
authenticity only results in a pummeling by a highly indignant
gorilla, to the amusement of several million television watchers.

Frank is an antihero, *his* lion of stone is the Denfert-Rochereau monument in Paris, the end of his quest is a cage in the Jardin des Plantes. In essence, Frank's quest turns out to be a flight from responsibility. He needs to escape complicity for the deaths of Mr. Jolin and Tom. He knows that his wife is superior to him, and so justifies his hostility toward her by pretending she is a witch. Frank simply is unable to make responsible decisions. It had always been that way with him. His nonsense word games represented his "art," parodying his escape through creativity. Only when Frank returns to the land and decides to devote himself to Kamma's child does it appear that he has left Nobiskro behind. This is a far, far cry from Mrs. Frisaksen's advice to Wilfred, or Matias Roos's solution, or that of the climber in *Den røde tåken*. Frank has found his way out by *facing up* to the problems of existence. It is diametrically opposed to the artist's means of transforming them.

Is Borgen then repudiating, or at least reexamining, his earlier work? Does he now tell us that art is what permits the artist to escape his genuine responsibilities to life? Kamma's news reporting prevails over Frank's word puzzles, Molineux's simple wisdom prevails over Villon, and the Frenchman transmits his truths through personal contact rather than through any art form. We must not forget, however, that autocriticism has always been an essential part of Borgen's work, and whatever "solutions" he once proposed must later be seen as merely tentative. In 1962 he said of Branner: "*He* doesn't spare himself." And he continued: "But Branner also teaches us that childhood within the adult may become a vice, an escape. It is risky to *playact* one's life, in 'innocent' flight from seriousness and responsibility. Transformed into vice, it becomes a game lacking innocence! In such a game his [Branner's] people may risk giving free play to their egoism—that unrestricted egoism and self-centeredness of the child. In the adult this represents a danger for other human beings."[10] These words surely apply to Borgen's protagonists. The quests of Wilfred, Matias, Peter, and of course Frank are suffused with egocentricity and hurt others. Borgen is an artist who is painfully aware of the dangers of the artistic quest.

While *Min arm, min tarm* does not indicate a change of direction in the evolution of Borgen's thought, it nonetheless transmits a new feeling of impatience. At seventy, Borgen may believe that his own time has become too precious for games. He may as well be impatient with critics who have failed to see the anguished groping for answers within his work. Our civilization is in desperate need of acts. No longer can it afford the luxury of an elite shying away from social involvement in order to indulge itself in abstract quests for personal identity. In *Min arm, min tarm* Borgen reverts to a style resembling the "mumle gåsegg" he produced more than thirty years earlier: "A summer has passed. One more. That's the thing about summers, people don't quite know what happened to them. The atmosphere becomes melancholy as soon as the leaves start falling and the air begins to smell like snow. Some think it is the final summer. That's because the waves haven't yet settled since the Environment Congress in Stockholm, where spokesmen for industry and progress agreed that it would be too costly to save the world."[11]

It is the world, not the individual, that is in need of being saved. The individual must cease circling around his past and concentrate upon humanity's future. At the same time he must deflate his ego. In *Min arm, min tarm* the questing hero was exposed and punished through ridicule. The humiliation helped him to shake loose from his psychological anguish and he learned to revel in the simple. The cynicism of a Wilfred or Matias, based as it was upon an overblown notion of one's own significance, must yield to an uncomplicated confidence in the goodwill of others. This is what Borgen calls the "antirevolutionary revolution."[12]

Interpreted in another way, Borgen's fiction reveals the author's struggle to liberate himself from a literary tradition he has inherited. After the publication of *Mot mørket* in 1925, Borgen deplored what he called his "unhappy talent for imitation."[13] Borgen's mature work bears a profound mark of the author's readings. This, of course, does not indicate a lack of originality, but rather shows a preoccupation with broad, universal themes. Borgen is steeped in a literary tradition whose first modern exponent was François Villon, but whose roots lie in the mythologies of the Hebrews and the Greeks. This tradition has produced splendid works of art, works which have given stark definitions of man's exile in the world and his longing for absolutes he cannot grasp. Significant nineteenth- and twentieth-century writers, while continuing the tradition, frequently express anguished complaints about having nothing new to say about the human condition. In our time, this feeling is common among novelists. For many, the novel can only renew itself through a quest for new forms. Tired of the myths of man's tragic condition, some feel that the time has come to dehumanize the novel in favor of razor-sharp descriptions of the objects that surround us. Like Beckett, others actually attempt to transform their anguish of having nothing new to say into material for original works.

Borgen's concern for form is evident, particularly in *"Jeg"* and *Den røde tåken*. The problem of originality does, moreover, form a significant theme in his novels. His protagonists are all individuals with great appetites, "Mumle Gåseggs" of sorts. Borgen frequently compares them to blood-sucking vampires. The result is degradation, not of the vampire, but of its victim. This theme takes on added significance when the source of nourishment is literary or artistic. A quote from *Blåtind* may help illuminate the problem: "What happens to a trite tune, a theme which is continuously imitated, stolen, assimilated into a foreign musical organism? What happens to the original motif is that it nauseates us, we find it cheap and banal, we recognize it in all that is second-rate, and then we blame *it*.[14] What Borgen seems to be saying with increasing urgency is that the novel has reached a stage in its development where it can no longer afford to lean wholly on tradition. In fact, by continuing to re-create the old myths in new dress, we risk degrading the originals. Moreover, the time has come to start reexamining the content of the myths upon which so many of our literary works are built. Do the patterns they force us into really respond to the needs of our time? When Peter Holmgren started to suspect that his map did not match the landscape, he would instinctively trust the map more than he would trust his own eyes. He perished because he changed his course too late. The revolution Borgen proposes is profound. It would involve a complete reevaluation of our literary heritage, so as to liberate us from the circles of the past and enable us to start mapping out a new, more realistic course for the future.

Notes and References

Preface

1. Kjell Heggelund, *Fiksjon og virkelighet. En studie i tre nordiske jeg-romaner* (Oslo, 1966), pp. 73–101. Kjell Berger, "Flukten fra Nobiskro," in *Johan Borgen 1902–1962*, ed. Martin Synnes and Jan Erik Vold (Oslo, 1962), pp. 55–80.

2. Leif Longum, *Et speil for oss selv. Menneskesyn og virkelighetsoppfatning i norsk etterkrigsprosa* (Oslo, 1968), pp. 206–20.

3. Willy Dahl, *Stil og struktur. Utviklingslinjer i norsk prosa gjennom 150 år* (Oslo, 1965), p. 123.

Chapter One

1. Johan Borgen, *Barndommens rike* (Oslo, 1968), p. 18. This edition of *Barndommens rike* was published by Den Norske Bokklubben. The information I give about Borgen's childhood is largely taken from this volume.

2. *Ibid.*, p. 123.

3. *Ibid.*, p. 185.

4. Erling Nielsen, "Efterskrift," in Johan Borgen, *129 Mumle Gåsegg*, ed. Erling Nielsen (Oslo, 1971), p. 180. In this excellent edition of Borgen's "Mumle Gåsegg," Nielsen gives valuable information about the author's career as a journalist. I wish to recognize my debt to Nielsen's study.

5. Ragnar Vold, "Mumle Gåsegg," in *Johan Borgen 1902–1962*, p. 54. See also *129 Mumle Gåsegg*, p. 181.

6. *129 Mumle Gåsegg*, p. 182.

7. Personal interview with Borgen, June, 1972.

8. Leif Longum, *Et speil for oss selv*, pp. 216–18. Kjell Heggelund, *Fiksjon og virkelighet*, pp. 73–101.

9. The radio talks were selected and edited by Haagen Ringnes.

Chapter Two

1. *129 Mumle Gåsegg*. Two previous editions of Borgen's short articles from *Dagbladet* exist: *Betraktninger og anfektelser* (Oslo, 1932), and *60 Mumle Gåsegg* (Oslo, 1936).

2. *129 Mumle Gåsegg*, p. 172.

3. For the sake of readability, in the text I give only the English equivalent of the Norwegian title of Borgen's brief articles. In the footnotes I give the original Norwegian titles. I am using Nielsen's list of dates.

4. "Omkring begivenheten." *129 Mumle Gåsegg*, p. 34.

5. "I det små." *Ibid.*, pp. 38–39.

6. "Krig." *Ibid.*, p. 73.

7. "Oppvåkning." *Ibid.*, p. 74.

8. The Norwegian word *pris* means both *prize* and *price*. Borgen is making a play on words impossible to translate into English.

9. "Sett på dansemusikken." *129 Mumle Gåsegg*, p. 76.

10. "Virkeligheter." *Ibid.*, p. 112.

11. "Aprildag." *Ibid.*, p. 117.

12. "Reklamenotis for et kart." *Ibid.*, p. 125.

13. "I nummer ti." *Ibid.*, pp. 128–29. My interpretation of this piece follows that of Nielsen. See *129 Mumle Gåsegg*, pp. 185–86.

14. "Om sopp." *129 Mumle Gåsegg*, p. 172.

15. "I det små." *Ibid.*, p. 175. While the article is about Monaco, it is clearly Norway Borgen has in mind.

16. Johan Borgen, *Ord gjennom år*, ed. Erling Nielsen (Oslo, 1966), pp. 54–56.

17. Johan Borgen, *Alltid på en søndag*, ed. Haagen Ringnes (Oslo, 1968), pp. 36–38.

18. *Ibid.*, p. 105.

19. *Ibid.*, p. 152.

20. *Ibid.*, p. 169.

21. *Ord gjennom år*, p. 132.

22. *Ibid.*, p. 169.

23. *Barndommens rike*, p. 190.

24. *Ord gjennom år*, p. 150.

25. *Ibid.*, p. 152.

26. *Ibid.*, p. 156.

27. *Ibid.*, p. 163.

28. *Ibid.*, p. 162. Borgen's italics.

29. *Ibid.*, p. 156.

30. *Ibid.*, p. 181.

31. *Ibid.*, p. 182.

32. This, of course, does not mean that Borgen's protagonists are identical with their author or even necessarily his spokesmen. It simply means that the conflicts and themes in the works are essential for the author himself.

33. *Ord gjennom år*, p. 197.

34. Å leve—er krig med trolle / i hjertets og hjernens hvelv, Å dikte,—det er å holde / dommedag over seg selv.

35. *Ord gjennom år*, p. 196.

36. *Ibid.*, p. 203.

Chapter Three

1. Johan Borgen, *Innbilningen og kunsten* (Oslo, 1966), pp. 9–13. Reprinted from *Innbilningens verden* (Oslo, 1960), pp. 50–54.

2. The description of the border guards' refusal to accept the protagonist's passport reappears frequently in Borgen's work. It seems to be inspired by the scene in *The Trial* where the accusers ignore Joseph K.'s identification papers. See *Fiksjon og virkelighet*, pp. 87–88. Borgen discusses Kafka in *Innbilningens verden*, pp. 25–27; pp. 30–31.

3. *Innbilningens verden*, p. 53.

4. *Ibid.*, pp. 63–64. Borgen warns that a purely contemplative circling around the self does not necessarily bring man into closer contact with his authentic personality. The line of communication is established when the individual least expects it. The effect is that of Proust's "involuntary memory." Longum sees a vague relationship between Borgen's *ur-jeg* and Jung's archetypes. See *Et speil for oss selv*, p. 214.

5. *Innbilningens verden*, p. 71.

6. *Ibid.*, p. 54.

7. *Ibid.*, p. 26. The influence of Kierkegaard seems obvious.

8. According to Friedrich Kluge, the word Nobiskro means "a house on the frontier." It was used during the Reformation in the sense of Purgatory. *Etymologisches Wörterbuch der Deutschen Sprache* (Berlin, 1963), pp. 512–13.

Chapter Four

1. Borgen's idea of the source of the self brings to mind the Hindu belief in a universal soul which the individual hopes to rejoin once he is liberated from the prison of time and space. While several of the ideas in the short stories appear similar to those found in Indian scripture, I have been unable to trace any direct influence. The mystical strain gradually disappears from Borgen's work.

2. Johan Borgen, *Noveller i utvalg 1936–1961* (Oslo, 1966), p. 42.

3. *Ibid.*, p. 43. The fish image reinforces the link between the boy and Christ. *Ichthýs*, fish, was the symbol of the early Christians. The letters stand for "Jesus — Christ — God — Son — Savior."

4. *Ibid.*

5. *Ibid.*, p. 99.

6. *Ibid.*, p. 284.

7. *Ibid.*, p. 287. The young couple brings to mind the youthful happiness of Einar and Agnes in Ibsen's *Brand*. The meeting with the somber, severe pastor affects Agnes in the same way as the darkness marks the young girl in "En klar dag i mai."

8. *Noveller i utvalg*, p. 287.

9. Johan Borgen, *Nye noveller* (Oslo, 1966), p. 97.

10. *Ibid.*, p. 103.

11. The myth of Theseus in the labyrinth serves as the source of the image of the individual lost in a maze of stone. In the Greek myth Ariadne, out of love for the hero, saved him from certain death in the labyrinth. Theseus fled with Ariadne, but later abandoned her.

12. *Noveller i utvalg*, p. 309.

13. *Ibid.*, p. 313. Borgen's italics.

14. *Nye noveller*, p. 30.

15. *Ibid.*, p. 37.

16. *Noveller i utvalg*, p. 338. The drowning boy is a prototype for many a Borgen protagonist, most notably Wilfred Sagen in the *Lillelord* trilogy.

17. *Ibid.*, p. 339.

18. *Ibid.*, p. 340.

19. *Nye noveller*, p. 49.

20. In his discussion of Borgen, Leif Longum points out the transitory nature of love in the author's work. While love provides timeless moments, it holds no promise of permanent happiness. See *Et speil for oss selv*, p. 215.

Chapter Five

1. H. C. Branner, "Den Uundværlige Digter." Address at the University of Oslo November 17, 1962. *Vinduet*, XVII, 1 (1963), 22.

2. Johan Borgen, *Nordahl Grieg* (Oslo, 1945), p. 32.

3. In his article, "Tid, miljø og historisk bakgrunn i Johan Borgens *Lillelord*," Ole Christian Lagesen discusses the historical background for the novel. *Edda*, LXX, 1 (1970), 17–27.

4. *Nordahl Grieg*, p. 30.

5. Johan Borgen, *De mørke kilder* (Oslo, 1969), p. 35. I have used the edition of the *Lillelord* trilogy (*Lillelord*, *De mørke kilder*, *Vi har ham nå*) published by Den Norske Bokklubben.

6. In the Norwegian the name Wilfred is a homonym for *vil fred*, literally "wants peace."

7. Borgen was probably inspired by H. C. Andersen's story about the live and artificial nightingales. Borgen recognizes H. C. Andersen

as an important influence. Interview, June, 1972. In the preface to the Russian translation of *Lillelord*, K. Teljatnikov calls Borgen's novel a parody of Frances H. Burnett's *Little Lord Fauntleroy*. See "Om Lillelord-trilogien," *Vinduet*, XXIV, 3 (1970), 172. In *Lillelord* (Oslo, 1967), p. 10, Borgen refers to Burnett's work.

8. *Lillelord*, p. 47. Wilfred's thirst for experiences of all kinds and his fear of involvement bring to mind the characters of André Gide.

9. *De mørke kilder*, p. 155.

10. Jean-Paul Sartre, *Les Mots* (Paris, 1964), p. 70.

11. *De mørke kilder*, p. 206.

12. Borgen readily acknowledges *Hamlet*'s influence on his work. In *Vi har ham nå* (Oslo, 1970), pp. 235–36, he includes several quotations in English from Shakespeare's play. Edvard Beyer notes the importance of the quest for a father in the trilogy. See "Bøkene om Lillelord," in *Johan Borgen 1902–1962*, p. 85.

13. Karl Philipp Moritz (1756–1793) was a German novelist associated with the *Sturm und Drang* movement. Borgen may have had Moritz in mind when he chose the name for his German officer.

14. *Vi har ham nå*, p. 89.

15. *De mørke kilder*, pp. 231, 245.

16. *Vi har ham nå*, p. 146.

17. *Ibid.*, p. 161. Borgen's italics.

18. *Ibid.*, p. 121.

19. *Fri* means "free." The significance of the name is obvious, since Wilfred's quest for Mrs. Frisaksen is a quest for freedom.

20. *Lillelord*, p. 129.

21. *Ibid.*

22. *Ibid.*, p. 148. Borgen's italics.

23. *De mørke kilder*, p. 216.

24. *Ibid.*, p. 254.

25. *Ibid.*, p. 255.

26. *Ibid.*, p. 258.

27. *Vi har ham nå*, p. 205.

28. *Ibid.*, p. 178.

29. *Ibid.*, p. 212.

30. *Ibid.*, p. 242. Once again the comparison between Wilfred and the drowning dog seems appropriate.

Chapter Six

1. Kjell Heggelund discusses the literary allusions in *"Jeg."* See *Fiksjon og virkelighet*, pp. 87–93.

2. Swann's dream at the end of *Du Côté de chez Swann* follows the same basic pattern: splitting up of the personality into an active and a passive part, acting out of the conflict, reintegration of the personality, and liberation. *A la Recherche du temps perdu*, Pléiade edition (Paris, 1954), I, 378–82.

3. Johan Borgen, *"Jeg"* (Oslo, 1959), p. 241. Kjell Berger compares the relationship between "I" and "he" in *"Jeg"* to that of Nagel and the Midget in Hamsun's *Mysteries*. See "Flukten fra Nobiskro," in *Johan Borgen 1902–1962*, p. 57.

4. In this case Borgen adheres to the literal meaning of the word Nobiskro, namely "house on the frontier." See p. 159, note 8.

5. *"Jeg,"* p. 204.

6. *Ibid.,* p. 187.

7. Joseph K. in *The Trial* is such a stranger figure. So are Nagel in *Mysteries* and the protagonist of *Pan*, Thomas Glahn.

8. *"Jeg,"* p. 10. "Flukten fra Nobiskro," in *Johan Borgen 1902–1962*, p. 79.

9. *"Jeg,"* p. 26.

10. Heggelund points out that Mrs. Skarseth's problems reflect those of Matias himself. She therefore becomes a kind of caricature of the protagonist. *Fiksjon og virkelighet*, p. 76. My own interpretation of *"Jeg"* is indebted to Heggelund's.

11. *"Jeg,"* p. 68.

12. This episode recurs frequently in Borgen's work.

13. The episode of the English chair also recurs several times in Borgen's work. Borgen is a master at evoking how old houses can stimulate fantasy and dream. His descriptions could serve as illustrations to Bachelard's suggestive comments on "la maison onirique." See Pierre Quillet, *Bachelard* (Paris, 1964), pp. 211–14.

14. *"Jeg,"* p. 176.

15. *Ibid.,* p. 177.

16. *Ibid.* Berger calls Fartein a frustrated incarnation of Matias's original innocence. See "Flukten fra Nobiskro," in *Johan Borgen 1902–1962*, p. 66.

17. *"Jeg,"* p. 181.

18. *Ibid.,* p. 183. The desire of man to dominate his human condition by becoming an agent of destruction has a Nietzschean ring. The most famous example of this theme used in twentieth-century literature is perhaps Camus's *Caligula*. Borgen has much in common with Camus (the theme of alienation, the quest for a lost land, the duality between solitude and human solidarity), whom he, unjustly perhaps, considers to be a second-rate writer. See *Vinduet*, XI, 4 (1957), 246–47.

19. *"Jeg,"* p. 240. Borgen's italics.

20. *Ibid.,* p. 234.

21. *Fiksjon og virkelighet,* p. 110.

22. *"Jeg,"* p. 218.

23. *Ibid.,* p. 233. The extreme example of the hero who is unable to integrate his internal vision into external reality is Oblomov, the protagonist of Gontcharov's celebrated novel.

24. *Ibid.,* p. 236.

Chapter Seven

1. Johan Borgen, *Blåtind* (Oslo, 1964), p. 7.

2. *Ibid.,* p. 227.

3. *Ibid.,* p. 41. Borgen's italics.

4. *Ibid.,* p. 157.

5. *Ibid.,* p. 8.

6. *Ibid.,* pp. 51–62; pp. 65–75; pp. 198–212.

7. *Ibid.,* p. 200.

8. *Ibid.,* p. 209. Borgen's italics.

9. *Ibid.,* p. 210.

10. *Ibid.,* pp. 211–12.

11. The scene is similar to the one in the *Lillelord* trilogy where Wilfred lies down beside Mrs. Frisaksen's corpse.

12. *Blåtind,* p. 232.

13. *Vi har ham nå,* p. 241.

Chapter Eight

1. Interview with Borgen, June, 1972.

2. Johan Borgen, *Den røde tåken* (Oslo, 1967), p. 75.

3. *Ibid.,* p. 107.

4. *Ibid.,* p. 8.

5. *Ibid.,* pp. 9–10.

6. *Ibid.,* p. 38.

7. *Ibid.,* p. 44.

8. *Ibid.,* p. 99.

9. *Ibid.,* p. 100. Borgen's italics.

10. *Ibid.,* p. 52.

11. *Ibid.,* p. 96. Borgen's italics.

12. *Time,* December 4, 1972, pp. 32–35.

13. *Den røde tåken,* p. 116. While the quotation describes the memory of an experience the protagonist had in the past and therefore may seem to be lifted out of context, it nevertheless illustrates

the mood of the final section of the novel with great precision. The protagonist repeatedly experiences the "fall" as a birth, or rebirth, through cleansing. See pp. 104, 128.

14. *Den røde tåken*, p. 114.

15. *Ibid.*, p. 137.

16. Sophocles, *Oedipus the King*, in *The Complete Greek Tragedies*, vol. III, ed. David Grene and Richmond Lattimore. Modern Library Edition (New York, n.d.), p. 77.

17. *Den røde tåken*, p. 72.

18. Northrop Frye, *Anatomy of Criticism* (Princeton, 1973), p. 150. (First edition, 1957).

19. On p. 61 of *Den røde tåken*, the protagonist thinks of his quest as a journey toward the center of the sun, "where all is in the same instant consumed—" This reference brings to mind Icarus, whose wings melted when he ventured too close to the sun. On p. 102 there is a reference to the giants who sought freedom before God's throne in the sky, "and were poorly rewarded for their pride."

20. *Den røde tåken*, p. 61.

21. Georges Poulet, *L'Espace proustien* (Paris, 1963), pp. 160–61.

22. The associations of solitude, height, and vision are frequent in Romantic literature; e.g., De Vigny's "Moses" on top of Mount Nebo, Stendhal's Fabrice del Dongo and Julien Sorel in their towers.

23. *Den røde tåken*, p. 94, contains references to a "leap of faith."

24. *"Jeg,"* p. 86.

Chapter Nine

1. Johan Borgen, *Trær alene i skogen* (Oslo, 1969), p. 173.

2. *Ibid.*, p. 147.

3. *Ibid.*, p. 57. In an interview with Jan Erik Vold, Borgen explains his longtime interest in Robert. In *Når alt kommer til alt* (1934) Robert had appeared as a secondary character, and Borgen once intended to write a novel with him as protagonist. See "Hovedperson / biperson. Johan Borgen i samtale med Jan Erik Vold," *Vinduet*, XXIV, 3 (1970), 175–77.

4. *Vi har ham nå*, p. 50.

5. Johan Borgen, *Min arm, min tarm* (Oslo, 1972), p. 27.

6. *Ibid.*, p. 39.

7. The descriptions of Frank's self-images seem to be inspired by Existentialist psychology. According to the Existentialists, the individual will see himself through the eyes of other people. Sartre studies this problem in his exhaustive work *Saint Genet* (Paris, 1952). According to Sartre, Genet became a thief and homosexual because

society had stamped him as such. While Borgen does not mention Sartre, in *Min arm, min tarm* he refers to the Existentialist psychologist R. D. Laing several times. Pp. 55, 65, 67, 69. Borgen may have been inspired by Laing's works, *The Divided Self* (Baltimore, Penguin Books, 1965. First edition London, 1960), and *Self and Others* (Baltimore, Pelican Books, 1971. First edition London, 1961).

8. *Min arm, min tarm*, p. 47.

9. *Ibid.*, p. 15.

10. *Ibid.*, p. 93.

11. *Ibid.*, p. 121.

12. *Ibid.*

13. *Ibid.*, p. 163.

14. *Ve - gård - hei* means literally "woe" - "farm" - "moor." Frank's story describes the "woe" of the Norwegian farm boy turned intellectual.

15. Sartre would have condemned this as an outrageous example of Frank's "bad faith."

16. An Existentialist would accuse Frank of turning other people into objects which he may use for his own ends.

17. *Min arm, min tarm*, p. 30. Wilfred used similar words in regard to Mrs. Frisaksen. He wished to become like her in order to avoid bothersome involvement with other people. Cf. p. 79.

18. *Min arm, min tarm*, p. 34.

19. *Ibid.*, p. 80.

20. *Ibid.*, pp. 88–89. Frank's mental distortion of Kamma into "something with teeth" is Kafkaesque. In *Vi har ham nå*, pp. 57–58, Wilfred mentioned a short story by Kafka, in which the population of a country was completely bewitched by the teeth of a group of otherwise harmless soldiers. The word Kamma contains the Norwegian word *kam* ("comb"), literally an object with teeth. The word-conscious Frank was certainly aware of this connection. See *Min arm, min tarm*, p. 162. Frank, like the family in Kafka's "The Metamorphosis," must rid himself of the mental distortions he has constructed before he can hope to return to a normal form of existence.

21. *Min arm, min tarm*, p. 127.

22. *Ibid.*, p. 137.

23. *Ibid.*, p. 136.

24. *Ibid.*, p. 127.

25. *Ibid.*, p. 132.

26. *Ibid.*, p. 199.

27. *Ibid.* p. 208.

28. The humorous title of the novel, *Min arm, min tarm*, with its

repetition of the possessive pronoun *min* ("my"), underscores the egoism of which Frank had to free himself in order to gain a sense of identity.

Chapter Ten

1. *Ord gjennom år,* p. 189.
2. T. S. Eliot, *Collected Poems 1909–1962* (New York, 1963), pp. 178–79. Quoted in Maurice Friedman, *To Deny Our Nothingness: Contemporary Images of Man* (New York, 1967), p. 92.
3. The comparisons with Beckett are meant merely to show some basic similarities in two contemporary writers, who in most respects are vastly different from one another. Above all, I do not intend to suggest any influence.
4. *Ord gjennom år,* p. 176. Borgen's italics.
5. See discussion of "Vinterhav," p. 60.
6. *Den røde tåken,* p. 31.
7. *Ibid.,* p. 90.
8. *Ibid.,* p. 93.
9. Earlier Borgen heroes used alcohol and other stimulants to help them escape reality. Matias, however, was sober when he told his story to Sonja; the protagonist in *Den røde tåken* was sober when he climbed to the top of the monolith.
10. *Ord gjennom år,* p. 199.
11. *Min arm, min tarm,* p. 193.
12. *Ibid.,* p. 145.
13. See p. 21.
14. *Blåtind,* p. 134. Borgen's italics.

Selected Bibliography

WORKS BY JOHAN BORGEN

Mot Mørket. Oslo: Gyldendal, 1925.

Betraktninger og anfektelser. Mumle Gåsegg [pseud.]. Oslo: Krag og Støle, 1932.

Når alt kommer til alt. Oslo: Gyldendal, 1934.

Lille dommedag. Jørgen Hattemaker [pseud.]. Oslo: Aschehoug, 1935.

Kontorsjef Lie. Oslo: Gyldendal, 1936.

Seksti Mumle Gåsegg. Mumle Gåsegg [pseud.]. Oslo: Gyldendal, 1936.

Barnesinn. Oslo: Gyldendal, 1937.

Høit var du elsket. Oslo: Gyldendal, 1937.

Mens vi venter. Oslo: Gyldendal, 1938.

Andersens. Oslo: Gyldendal, 1940.

Anes eventyr. Oslo: Johan Grundt Tanum, 1941–43.

Ingen sommar. Translated by Vanja Lantz. Stockholm: Norstedt & Söner, 1944. Published in Norwegian as *Ingen sommer.* Oslo: Gyldendal, 1946

Det nytter. Helge Lind [pseud.]. Translated by Barbro Alving. Stockholm: Norstedt & Söner, 1944.

Nordahl Grieg. Stockholm: Bonniers, 1944. Oslo: Gyldendal, 1945.

Dager på Grini. Oslo: Gyldendal, 1945.

Far, mor og oss. Mumle Gåsegg [pseud.]. Oslo: J. W. Cappelen, 1945.

Kjærlighetsstien. Oslo: Gyldendal, 1946.

Reidar Aulie. Oslo: Dreyer, 1946.

Akvariet. Oslo: Gyldendal, 1947.

Hvetebrødsdager. Oslo: Gyldendal, 1948.

Jenny og påfuglen. Oslo: Gyldendal, 1949.

Vikinger og eventyr. Oslo: Gyldendal, 1949.

Kunsten i Oslo rådhus. Oslo: Aschehoug, 1950.

Noveller om kjærlighet. Oslo: Gyldendal, 1952.

Natt og dag. Oslo: Gyldendal, 1954.

Lillelord. Oslo: Gyldendal, 1955. (Norwegian Book Club edition, 1967.)

De mørke kilder. Oslo: Gyldendal, 1956. (Norwegian Book Club edition, 1969.)

Vi har ham nå. Oslo: Gyldendal, 1957. (Norwegian Book Club edition, 1970.)
"Jeg." Oslo: Gyldendal, 1959.
Danmark dejligst?. Translated by Erling Nielsen. Copenhagen: H. Reitzel, 1960.
Innbilningens verden. Oslo: J. W. Cappelen, 1960.
Noveller i utvalg 1936–1961. Oslo: Gyldendal, 1961.
Frigjøringsdag. Oslo: Gyldendal, 1963.
Blåtind. Oslo: Gyldendal, 1964.
Barndommens rike. Oslo: Gyldendal, 1965. (Norwegian Book Club edition, 1968.)
Nye noveller. Oslo: Gyldendal, 1965.
Ord gjennom år. Oslo: Gyldendal, 1966.
Innbilningen og kunsten. Oslo: Aas and Wahls Boktrykkeri / Det Mallingske Boktrykkeri, 1966.
Bagateller. Oslo: Gyldendal, 1967.
Den røde tåken. Oslo: Gyldendal, 1967.
Alltid på en søndag. Edited by Haagen Ringnes. Oslo: Gyldendal, 1968.
Trær alene i skogen. Oslo: Gyldendal, 1969.
Elsk meg bort –. Oslo: Gyldendal, 1970.
Mitt hundeliv. Oslo: Gyldendal, 1971.
129 Mumle Gåsegg. Edited by Erling Nielsen. Oslo: Gyldendal, 1971.
Far, mor og oss. Oslo: Gyldendal, 1971.
Min arm, min tarm. Oslo: Gyldendal, 1972.
"Hovedperson / biperson." Interview with J. E. Vold. *Vinduet,* XXIV, 3 (1970), 175–80. Commentary by J. B., *ibid.,* 181–82.
Den store havfrue. Oslo: Gyldendal, 1973.

BIOGRAPHICAL AND CRITICAL STUDIES

AARSETH, ASBJØRN. "Genrebilde med epifani," in *Tekstopplevelser. Ni analyser av norske prosatekster.* Edited by Willy Dahl. Oslo: Universitetsforlaget, 1970, pp. 120–28.
BERGER, KJELL. "Flukten fra Nobiskro," in *Johan Borgen 1902–1962.* Edited by Martin Synnes and Jan Erik Vold. Oslo: Kulturutvalget i Det Norske Studentersamfund, 1962, pp. 55–80.
—————. "Vår nordiske lengsel," *Vinduet,* XVIII, 4 (1964), 308–12.
BIRN, RANDI MARIE. "The Quest for Authenticity in Three Novels by Johan Borgen," *Mosaic,* IV, 2 (1970), 91–99.
—————. "Dream and Reality in Johan Borgen's Short Stories," *Scandinavian Studies,* XLVI, 1 (1974), 57–72.

Selected Bibliography   169

BRANNER, HANS CHRISTIAN. "Den uundværlige digter," [Address at the University of Oslo, November 17, 1962], *Vinduet*, XVII, 1 (1963), 17–23.

BREKKE, PAAL. "Johan Borgens 'Jeg,'" *Samtiden*, LXVIII (1959), 518–23.

BRØNDSTED, MOGENS (ed.). *Nordens Litteratur Efter 1860*. Oslo: Gyldendal, 1972, pp. 516–19.

DAHL, WILLY. *Fra 40-tall til 60-tall. Norsk prosa gjennom 25 år*. Oslo: Gyldendal, 1969.

––––––. "Første møte med en romanfigur. Åpningssidene i Johan Borgens *Lillelord*," *Norsk Litterær Årbok*, 1 (1966), 136–42.

––––––. *Nytt norsk forfatterleksikon*. Oslo: Gyldendal, 1971, pp. 34–35.

––––––. *Stil og struktur. Utviklingslinjer i norsk prosa gjennom 150 år*. Oslo: Universitetsforlaget, 1965.

EHNMARK, ANDERS. "Forräderiets lust och kval," *Bonniers Litterära Magasin*, XXVII (1968), 45–50.

HEGGELUND, KJELL. *Fiksjon og virkelighet. En studie i tre nordiske jeg-romaner*. Oslo: Universitetsforlaget, 1966.

HERBJØRNSRUD, HANS. "Veien til Nobiskro. Dikterne og den første verdenskrig," *Samtiden*, LXXIII, 9 (1964), 527–40.

HOUM, PHILIP. *Norsk Litteraturhistorie*, Vol. VI. Oslo: Aschehoug, 1955.

HVENEKILDE, ANNE. *Om Johan Borgens noveller*. Oslo: Folkets Brevskole, 1968.

LAGESEN, OLE CHRISTIAN. "Tid, miljø og historisk bakgrunn i Johan Borgens *Lillelord*," *Edda*, LXX, 1 (1970), 17–27.

LONGUM, LEIF. *Et speil for oss selv. Menneskesyn og virkelighets-oppfatning i norsk etterkrigsprosa*. Oslo: Aschehoug, 1968.

MICHL, JOSEF B. "Franz Kafka und die moderne Skandinavische Literatur," *Schweizer Monatshefte für Politik, Wirtschaft, Kultur*, XLVIII, 1 (1968), 57–71.

RUNNQUIST, ÅKE. *Moderne nordiske forfattere*. Oslo: Chr. Schibsteds Forlag, 1967, pp. 185–87.

SCHULERUD, MENTZ. "Profilen: Johan Borgen," *Vinduet*, XIV, 2 (1960), 89–92.

SKIPENES, DAGFRID. "Identitetsproblemet i dikterisk belysning," *Vinduet*, VI, 1 (1961), 36–45.

SYNNES, MARTIN, and JAN ERIK VOLD (Eds.). *Johan Borgen 1902–1962*. Oslo: Kulturutvalget i Det Norske Studentersamfund, 1962.

TELJATNIKOV, K. "Om Lillelord-trilogien," *Vinduet*, XXIV, 3 (1970), 172–74. [From the introduction to the Russian translation of the novel, 1968.]

OTHER CRITICAL MATERIAL CITED IN THE TEXT

FRIEDMAN, MAURICE. *To Deny Our Nothingness. Contemporary Images of Man.* New York: Dell Publishing Co., 1967.

FRYE, NORTHROP. *Anatomy of Criticism.* Princeton: Princeton University Press, 1973.

KLUGE, FRIEDRICH. *Etymologisches Wörterbuch der Deutschen Sprache.* Berlin: W. de Gruyter, 1963.

LAING, R. D. *The Divided Self.* Baltimore: Penguin Books, 1965.

—————. *Self and Others.* Baltimore: Penguin Books, 1971.

POULET, GEORGES. *L'Espace proustien.* Paris: Gallimard, 1963.

QUILLET, PIERRE. *Bachelard.* Paris: Seghers, 1964.

SARTRE, JEAN-PAUL. *Saint Genet: Comédien et martyr.* Paris: Gallimard, 1952.

Index

171